PRO WRESTLING

PRO WRESTLING

From Carnivals to Cable TV

Keith Elliot Greenberg

LERNER
SPORTS
AN IMPRINT OF LERNER PUBLISHING GROUP

12680807

To Jennifer and Dylan Greenberg

Author Acknowledgments
The author wishes to thank the following people for their assistance
on this book: Cage Nakayama, Shun Yamaguchi, Vince Russo,
Dave Meltzer, Ed Riciutti, Jimmy Suzuki, Mike Weber, Dennis Brent,
Stu Miller, Lou Gianfriddo, Mike Mooneyham, Julie Jensen,
Michele Moore, Jim Byrne, and Alan Sharp.

This book is available in two editions:
Library binding by LernerSports
Soft cover by First Avenue Editions,
Imprints of Lerner Publishing Group
241 First Avenue North
Minneapolis, MN 55401 U.S.A.

Library of Congress Cataloging-in-Publication Data

Greenberg, Keith Elliot.
    Pro wrestling : from carnivals to cable TV / Keith Elliot
Greenberg.
        p.   cm.
        Includes bibliographical references and index.
        Summary: A history of professional wrestling from its roots in
    legitimate sport to its days as a carnival attraction followed by
    the growth of regional rivalries and culminating as television-
    centered entertainment.
        ISBN 0-8225-3332-4 (lib. bdg. : alk. paper)
        ISBN 0-8225-9864-7 (pbk. : alk. paper)
        1. Wrestling—History—Juvenile literature. [1. Wrestling.] I.
    Title.
    GV1195.3.G74   2000
    796.812—dc21   99-050554

Manufactured in the United States of America
1 2 3 4 5 6 – JR – 05 04 03 02 01 00

Contents

1 The War Zone 7

2 The Roots of
Pro Wrestling 11

3 Gorgeous George 23

4 Women's Wrestling . . .31

5 The Age of
Territories 37

6 Rock 'n' Wrestling 45

7 The Fight for Power . . .59

8 Japanese Pro Wrestling . .69

9 The Murder of
Bruiser Brody 81

10 Scandal 89

11 The New World Order . .97

12 Attitude 105

13 A Sad Farewell 117

Further Reading *126*
Index *127*

THE WAR ZONE

After the third referee of the match was knocked out, many of those watching the main event of "WrestleMania XV" stopped counting.

Since 1985, the World Wrestling Federation (WWF) had been staging this loud, flashy spectacular event every year—comparing it to football's Super Bowl. On March 28, 1999, the crowd at Philadelphia's First Union Center was on its feet, screaming as the WWF heavyweight champion, the Rock—a third-generation wrestler named Dwayne Johnson—and challenger Stone Cold Steve Austin laced into each other. In more than 850,000 homes, fans were also following the action on pay-per-view television.

Professional wrestling had never been hotter. Every Monday night, more than 10 million viewers watched the WWF and its rival, World Championship Wrestling (WCW), on two separate cable television networks. Soon, a third wrestling organization, Extreme Championship Wrestling (ECW), would run on a third cable network. Children played with wrestling action figures, competed against their friends at wrestling video games, and ate wrestling candy. Adults who claimed that

Opposite page: The Rock rode professional wrestling's wave of popularity to superstar status.

Pro Wrestling

Vince McMahon

their kids forced them to follow the explosive antics of performers like the Undertaker, Hulk Hogan, and Bret "Hit Man" Hart were frequently lying. People of every age, and from every background, loved professional wrestling.

This form of entertainment had come under fire, however. The critics claimed it was too violent. Women paraded around the ring in barely any clothing as the men in the audience whistled and hollered. Wrestlers used foul language while being interviewed in the ring and sometimes encouraged their fans to do the same. WCW representatives responded to these charges by claiming that their shows were cleaner and more "family friendly" than the WWF shows. Taking the opposite approach, WWF owner Vince McMahon noted that each time the media ran a negative story about professional wrestling—there were three in *The New York Times* on the morning of "WrestleMania XV"—his business increased.

For years, McMahon had admitted that the matches in the ring were not actual contests, like baseball and basketball games. He described the WWF as "sports entertainment"—a combination of athletics and theater. The point was putting on a good show so fans would keep watching. The feuds were not supposed to be taken too seriously. Those who felt outraged by the blood, the exposed flesh, and the folding chairs smashed across wrestlers' heads were told to remember that it was only wrestling.

To prove his point, McMahon had turned himself into professional wrestling's most hated villain, portraying himself as a mean boss who bullied everyone in his organization. When the fans booed him, it meant that McMahon was playing his role properly, just like a character in a movie or TV show.

On previous WWF broadcasts, McMahon had been at war with popular Stone Cold Steve Austin. During "WrestleMania XV," the WWF owner told viewers that he wanted to referee the main event and slant the match against the hero. Another referee started the bout, but he didn't last long. At one point, Austin swung a chair at his opponent. Instead of striking his foe, Austin appeared to hit, and knock out, the official. When the next referee made a call the Rock objected to, the champion drove the ref's head into the canvas. A third referee rushed into the ring and McMahon followed, attacking the official and stealing his spot.

Fans were now certain that Austin was going to lose, especially when McMahon helped the Rock stomp his opponent. But Mankind—a strange, bearded wrestler in a leather mask who, according to the WWF's announcers, also had a grudge against McMahon—saved the day.

Mankind delighted the crowd by throwing the owner of the World Wrestling Federation out of the ring. When Austin delivered his Stone Cold Stunner—a move that involves wrenching a man's neck—on the Rock, Mankind placed himself close to the action. As McMahon lay ringside with a frustrated look on his face, Austin pinned the champion's shoulders to the canvas for the three seconds required to win a match. Mankind dramatically slapped the mat three times, then awarded the championship to Austin. The arena rocked in cheers, while Austin—playing the part of a working guy who finally got the better of his cruel boss—punished McMahon with a Stone Cold Stunner and dumped beer on him.

Stone Cold Steve Austin

It seemed that no fan left the arena unhappy. "WrestleMania XV" had been everything the WWF had promised: unpredictable, exciting, and entertaining. The company had made millions of dollars from ticket sales, souvenir purchases, and pay-per-view orders. Even wrestling's harshest critics had to admit that, from a business point of view, the show was an enormous success.

However, one question remained. How did a sport included in the first Olympic Games—a contest that was supposed to symbolize the purest form of competition—turn into this?

2

The Roots of Pro Wrestling

Wrestling may be the world's only universal sport. In American Indian society—as well as the ancient cultures of Japan, Mexico, China, Turkey, and Egypt—humans have competed in battles of strength and skill.

Greek mythology is filled with tales of impressive wrestling matches among the gods, in particular, Hercules' battles with Ajax and Antaeus. For human participants, though, wrestling was extremely risky. Victory was often achieved only by killing the opponent—a custom that changed in about 900 B. C., when Theseus, the king of Athens, created a set of rules.

In the first and second centuries B. C., Greece fell under Roman conquest, and the Romans combined their style of wrestling with the Greek version. The result: Greco-Roman wrestling, which prohibits the combatants from applying holds below the waist. Greco-Roman wrestlers still compete on amateur levels and in the Olympics.

Wrestling as entertainment may have started in sixteenth century England, when matches were held

Opposite page: These figures were carved into an ancient Greek urn.

Works vs. Shoots

Almost all professional wrestling matches are works, exhibitions in which the participants know the ending before they ever step in the ring. But wrestlers are strong men with strong egos and, occasionally, the bouts turn into shoots—confrontations in which the violence is real.

Traditionally, every wrestling organization has had an enforcer, a legitimate tough guy who would target wrestlers who started to believe their own gimmicks of superstardom or who made trouble for promoters. When enforcers would square off against certain foes, the action would be "stiff." In other words, blows connected harder than in a typical pro wrestling match.

Allegedly, Mad Dog Buzz Sawyer played this role for Fritz Von Erich's World Class Wrestling Association in Texas, while Steve "Dr. Death" Williams punished his peers for Cowboy Bill Watts's Universal Wrestling Federation in Oklahoma. The Acolytes—Justin "Hawk" Bradshaw and Ron "Faarooq" Simmons—were rumored to have been World Wrestling Federation enforcers at least once in 1999.

In 1976, Japanese great Antonio Inoki was wrestling Akrum Pehelewan in his native Pakistan. The match was scheduled to be a work. But Pehelewan allegedly decided to overpower Inoki to score a victory in front of the stadium crowd of 40,000. Inoki is said to have defended himself by clamping an armbar on Pehelewan and applying pressure until his arm broke. Pehelewan committed suicide a short time afterward, supposedly because of the humiliation he suffered in the match.

During a 1987 Japanese tag team tournament, Riki Chosu, the most popular wrestler in his promotion at the time, had opponent Osamu Kido trapped in a leglock when another foe, Akira Maeda, stepped into the ring and delivered a legitimate kick to the hero's eye. Two bones in Chosu's face were broken. Taking advantage of the uproar, Maeda started a new promotion that he claimed would only feature shoots.

in a circus, which also featured acrobatic acts, clowns, and comedy routines. By this time, wrestlers had largely abandoned the Greco-Roman style for an anything-goes type of combat called "catch as catch can." By the early 1800s, England had a superstar wrestler, John Jordan, also known as the Devonshire Giant, who frequently kicked his opponent's legs until the foe could not continue.

In the 1830s, Irish immigrants imported wrestling to New England. They called this form of competition "collar and elbow" because a wrestler would begin his match with one hand on an opponent's shoulder, near the collar, and another just above his elbow. After the Civil War, this type of wrestling was presented at carnivals. The wrestlers assumed colorful names, costumes, and histories. A strongman would appear inside a tent, offering a cash prize to any local who could pin his shoulders to the mat for a count of three, or remain unbeaten for a period of 15 minutes. Some of the wrestlers were "hookers," men who could apply crippling, illegal holds called "hooks" to disable a tough opponent. Other times, the matches were "works" (fixed fights) as opposed to "shoots" (actual competitions). Occasionally, the "local yokel"—in reality, a member of the act dressed as a laborer or farmer—would thrill the crowd by beating the strongman in a "worked" match.

Mihaly Munkacsy painted The Wrestler's Challenge *sometime between 1900 and 1912.*

Pro Wrestling

These carnival wrestlers are trying to drum up business.

The carnival relationship to wrestling remains. Professional wrestlers communicate to each other in a secret tongue they call "carney" (a form of pig latin using Zs), the same language carnival employees use on the midway. There are also specific terms used by insiders in the wrestling business. A grappler cheered by fans is a "babyface," while a villain is a "heel." Blood is "juice," crowd reaction is "heat," and a wrestler who stirs up trouble behind the scenes is a "spoon." When a grappler loses a match, he "does the job." A man who goes down to defeat week after week is a "jobber."

—— Wrestling's Forefathers ——

A New York City policeman named William Muldoon emerged as the "father of American wrestling" at the end of the nineteenth century. Muldoon, who also boxed, engaged in both Greco-Roman and catch-as-catch-can bouts, sometimes leaving the dressing room dressed as a Roman gladiator. Despite his flashy appearance and billing as champion, Muldoon's matches could be boring. In 1880, he wrestled Professor William Miller to a draw in a match that took nine hours and 35 minutes.

The next year, Muldoon battled Clarence Whistler for nearly seven hours. At about 4 A. M., after most of the fans had left their seats, the promoter ended the match by ordering the lights turned off.

Wrestling's first "match of the century" was held at the Dexter Park Pavilion in Chicago in 1908, pitting heavyweight titlist Frank Gotch against the Russian Lion, George Hackenschmidt. Many sportswriters favored Hackenschmidt, the master of a bone-crunching bear hug. After two hours of tussling, Gotch got behind his opponent, gripped him around the waist, and threw him to the mat. Before Gotch could move in for a pin, Hackenschmidt quit. Hackenschmidt claimed that Gotch had soaked his body with oil for the match, preventing his foe from effectively applying holds, and used a number of illegal maneuvers, including headbutts and closed fists.

Three years later, the two were scheduled to wrestle again at Chicago's new Comiskey Park, the home of baseball's White Sox. But before the match, Gotch installed a hooker named Ad Santell in Hackenschmidt's training camp. During a sparing session, Santell purposely injured the challenger's knee. When Hackenschmidt asked promoters to postpone the match, they came up with a compromise. The match was scheduled as a two-out-of-three-fall contest. The winner would be the man who could pin his opponent or make him submit to a painful hold twice. Gotch pledged to lose one fall if Hackenschmidt kept his injury a secret. The Russian Lion agreed to the terms, but was double-crossed in the match when Gotch pinned him in two straight falls.

When reporters learned about the circumstances of the match, many stopped covering wrestling as a sport. Gotch didn't seem to mind. He joined a circus and did a wrestling act for the spectators.

At this point, promoters began copying techniques from vaudeville to keep spectators interested. A hooded wrestler called the Masked Marvel appeared. Promoter Toots Mondt—a former hooker notorious for viciously beating his wrestlers in the dressing room if they didn't follow his orders—started producing a packaged show. He sent the same

The Roots of Pro Wrestling

William Muldoon

Frank Gotch, left, and George Hackenschmidt shake hands before their match.

wrestlers to town after town to wrestle the same matches. He also introduced time limits, so fans would no longer be forced to watch tiresome, seven-hour bouts. Instead of endlessly exchanging holds while lying on the mat, wrestlers were encouraged to use moves like the flying dropkick, which consisted of a wrestler leaping off the mat to batter an opponent with both feet.

As professional wrestling became more show business and less sport, wrestlers went to great lengths to make their worked matches look believable. When a grappler threw a punch, he tried to connect using a forearm instead of a fist, softening the blow. Kicks landed on the shoulder, stomach, or arm, instead of the head. A man diving on a foe from the ropes actually grazed the man with a knee or elbow, rather than landing on him directly and causing injury. To make a bout more dramatic, both wrestlers had to work together, with the victim screaming and shaking in agony—"selling" his opponent's maneuvers.

The dominant wrestler of the 1920s was Ed "Strangler" Lewis, a Wisconsin native named Robert Herman Julius Friedlich, who borrowed his ring name from a star of the late 1800s, Evan "Strangler" Lewis. Lewis's specialty was his headlock. He told reporters that he perfected the hold by practicing on a wooden head: "It was split down the center, the two halves connected by powerful steel springs. To increase the power of my grip, I carried this gadget with me, and worked on it for hours, until I developed a grip that could crack a skull."

Lewis, his manager Billy Sandow, and promoter Toots Mondt tried ruling professional wrestling by combining their talents. Lewis was awarded the world championship four times. He was willing to

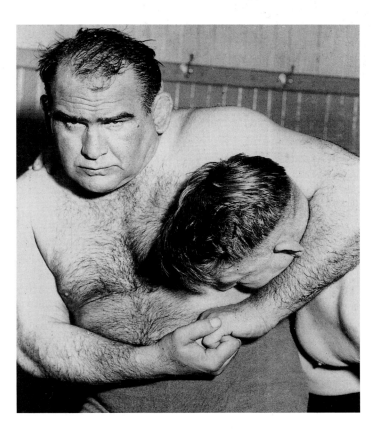

Ed "Strangler" Lewis demonstrates his signature move.

lose a match when he believed it was good for business. But no matter who wore the belt, the title always belonged to Lewis, Sandow, and Mondt—the Goldust Trio. Lewis was a tough shooter, a man who could really wrestle when it was necessary. If an opponent refused to lose to him in a worked match, Lewis would beat him legitimately.

Over time, though, the fans grew tired of watching Lewis. By the early 1930s, the United States was suffering through the Great Depression, and fewer Americans wanted to spend their hard-earned dollars on wrestling tickets. But professional wrestling managed to stay in business with promoters inventing new gimmicks to lure fans to the arenas.

—— *Unforgettable Personalities* ——

One of the first wrestling gimmicks was the tag team match, in which two teams of wrestlers square off. The first tag team match was held in San Francisco in 1901, but the concept didn't gain popularity until 1937, when Houston promoter Morris Sigel staged a "Texas Tornado" bout. Four wrestlers—Milo Steinborn and Whiskers Savage teamed against Tiger Daula and Fazul Mohammed—fought in the ring at the same time. Later, the rules were changed so that only two men could wrestle at once, while their partners watched from opposite corners of the ring. When the combatants wanted a break, they had to "tag out" to their teammates.

In 1938, Joe Reno and Roughhouse Ross wrestled in a ring filled with ice cream in Minneapolis. Promoters went on to present matches in mud, berries, and molasses. When wrestlers claimed to truly hate each other, they'd settle feuds wearing brass knuckles, shackled to one another with a chain, or locked inside a steel cage.

But gimmicks alone weren't enough. Promoters also needed strong personalities to draw crowds. Starting in the 1920s, professional wrestling recruited numerous college football stars. Wayne Munn from the University of Nebraska beat Strangler Lewis for the

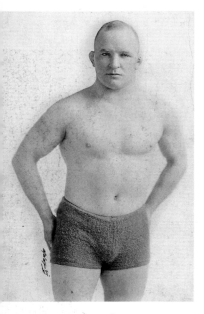

Toots Mondt

championship in 1925. Gus Sonnenberg of Dartmouth College and the University of Detroit won the belt four years later. Bronko Nagurski, an all-pro football player with the Chicago Bears, left the gridiron to become a wrestling star in the 1930s because, he said, the money was better.

Then there was Jim Londos, wrestling's "Golden Greek," a two-time world champion who some say saved professional wrestling as it struggled through the Depression. Londos, born Chris Theophelos in Argos, Greece, started wrestling in the United States during World War I, using his real name and wearing working clothes and shoes smeared with plaster. His

Jim Londos grapples with some young fans.

character was the "wrestling plasterer," a regular, hard-working guy, like the ones in the audience. When promoter Ed White told Theophelos his name was too difficult to pronounce, the wrestler picked an identity inspired by the surname of his favorite author, Jack London.

Like Hulk Hogan a half century later, Londos was respected by his opponents for "taking care" of them. No matter how brutal a match appeared, Londos did his best to make sure his foes felt as little pain as possible. "There was nobody like Chris," said rival Herman Hickman. "He could rip your arm from its socket, and you'd never know he had laid a hand on you."

In 1931, after wrestling Ray Steele for more than an hour at New York's Yankee Stadium, Londos locked his arms around his opponent's neck and won the match by appearing to put him to sleep. Londos described the move as "simply a new hold I've perfected which shuts off the jugular vein." Virtually every wrestling show uses Londos's "sleeper hold" to this day.

Londos was among the first of professional wrestling's ethnic heroes, men of foreign ancestry who told fans they were willing to suffer a punishing toll to achieve success in America. In the decades to come, Italy's Bruno Sammartino, Puerto Rico's Pedro Morales, and Poland's Ivan Putski would fall into the same category.

But first the wrestling world would celebrate Lou Thesz, the son of a Hungarian shoemaker from St. Louis. Thesz's father, who wrestled in amateur Greco-Roman competitions in Europe, began training him at age eight. By the time he was a teenager, Thesz had a reputation in St. Louis as a tough amateur. One day, Thesz's coach introduced him to Strangler Lewis. According to legend, the youngster pinned the wrestling champion in 22 seconds. But the story, like so much else in pro wrestling, is a work.

"Nobody in the world ever pinned him in 22 seconds," Thesz said. "We did work out in St. Louis, and he beat me—good."

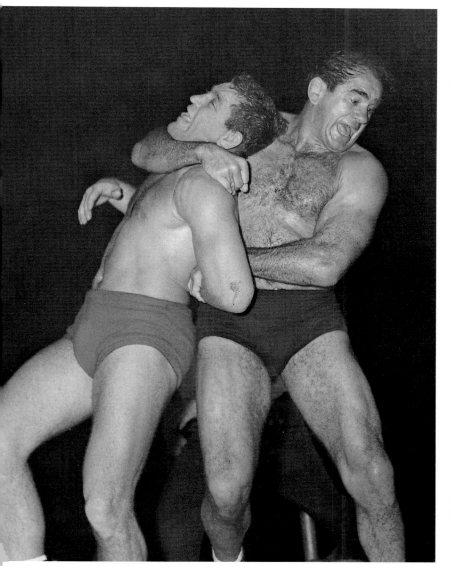

Danny Hodge, left, and Lou Thesz tangle.

Seeing Thesz's moneymaking potential, Lewis offered to take charge of the teenager's training and management. On December 29, 1937, the investment paid off. At age 21, Thesz captured the world championship from Everrett Marshall at the Kiel Auditorium in St. Louis. Thesz would continue wrestling until he was in his 70s and win the title another five times.

3

Gorgeous George

The years after World War II were very successful for American professional wrestling. Television was becoming popular, but networks needed programming. Taking advantage of the situation, wrestling promoters began providing tapes of matches to new stations in an effort to attract viewers to upcoming events, frequently referred to as "cards." In 1951, for example, fans in Los Angeles could watch wrestling every weeknight and Saturday afternoon, in addition to wrestlers' workouts on Sunday mornings.

There were many big stars during this era. Wladek "Killer" Kowalski was a powerful villain whose dramatic television interviews could provoke fans into a ticket-buying frenzy. Verne Gagne was a sensational college athlete who said he chose wrestling after rejecting offers from football's Cleveland Browns and Chicago Bears. The French Angel was a freakish-looking bald man with a large head, who had once allegedly pulled a New York City subway car with his teeth. The Sheik portrayed himself as a maniac from the Middle East, wearing a kaffiyeh, the headdress worn in Arab countries, and attacking opponents with weapons hidden in the trunks he wore.

Opposite page: Gorgeous George in all his finery. Above: Killer Kowalski was one of Gorgeous George's rivals.

Yet, even in this cast of colorful personalities, the wrestler known as Gorgeous George stood out from the pack. Although he was an average athlete, his flair for performance was perfectly suited to the television age.

——— *The Gorgeous One* ———

George Raymond Wagner was born March 24, 1915, in Seward, Nebraska. George grew up in Houston, Texas, in a tough neighborhood near the ship channel called Harrisburg. He later told reporters that he liked fighting and would purposely encourage other children to pick on him. "When I walked down the street, I wanted people to notice me," he said. "I used to wear knickers so the other kids would tease me and pick a fight."

George claimed that when he was nine, he looked at George Washington's picture on a dollar bill and noticed that the president had long hair, and at that moment, he decided to grow out his locks.

George had little appreciation for education, preferring to spend his time with a group of rough neighborhood kids called the Harrisburg Rats. Interestingly, several members of the gang—Chester Hayes, Sterling "Dizzy" Davis, and Jesse and Johnny James—later became wrestlers. Two other friends, Jack Hunter and Jake Brown, would become Gorgeous George's valets.

Verne Gagne

The Harrisburg Rats trained at the Houston YMCA and wrestled each other in the sawdust behind the fruit stand owned by the father of the James brothers. If anyone wanted to watch, the boys charged admission. At 17, after dropping out of Milby High School, George earned 35 cents for wrestling against an older man at a carnival. When the match was over, George saw his YMCA coach in the audience and walked up to shake his hand.

"You're not an amateur any more," the coach informed his student. "You're a professional."

George began wrestling as the Barefoot Bohemian at the Harrisburg Arena, Milby Arena, and other small halls on the edges of Houston. In 1938, at age 22, he won his first title, beating Buck Lipscomb for the Northwest middleweight championship in Eugene, Oregon. At that stage of his career, George tried getting the fans to boo him by entering the ring in spats and a fancy hat and carrying a walking stick. The gimmick didn't work, but George kept trying.

In 1939, he married Betty Hanson, a cashier at a Eugene movie theater, in the middle of the ring in her hometown. The fans enjoyed the event so much that the couple restaged the wedding several more times at arenas around the country. George made Betty professional wrestling's first female valet when, before one match, she accompanied him to the ring and carefully folded his robe. "The fans got on him pretty good, and Betty was there and got into it with the fans," Don Owen, the promoter in Oregon at the time, told author Joe Jares in his book, *Whatever Happened to Gorgeous George?* "She slapped one of them, and George went out of the ring, and belted the fan. . . . Anyway, the booing was tremendous and the next week, there was a really big crowd and everybody booed George. So he just took more time to fold his robe. He did everything to antagonize the fans. And from that point on, he became the best drawing card we ever had around here. In wrestling, they either come to like you or to hate you. And they hated George."

Gorgeous Antics

Once the fans started reacting to him, George became even more outrageous. He started calling himself Gorgeous George, even legally changing his name in 1950. He dyed his brown hair blond and held the long, curly locks in place with gold-colored bobby pins, called "Georgie Pins," before tossing the items to the crowd. To special friends, George gave 14-karat versions of the hair clasps. But before anyone could receive this gift, the person had to take an oath: "I do solemnly swear and promise to never

Gorgeous George

confuse this gold Georgie Pin with a common, ordinary bobby pin, so help me, Gorgeous George."

Before his matches, George walked across a red carpet to the ring, as the graduation song "Pomp and Circumstance" played over the loudspeaker. The ring announcer then declared that "the human orchid, the sensation of the nation, the toast of the coast" had arrived. George had both male and female valets throughout his career, and they always made a big production of spraying the ring with perfume, held in a jar called "the atomizer." George claimed that he'd once gotten an infection from wrestling on dirty mats and that the atomizer contained a special disinfectant. It was more likely that the wrestler was purposely acting fussy in order to get the fans to hate him more than they already did. In many cities, George brought a candelabra to the ring, extinguishing the flames with his pinkies.

As the bout started, the 210-pound athlete would act hesitant about having to touch his opponent's "dirty" body. When the referee searched George's boots and trunks for hidden weapons, the wrestler would scream, "Take your filthy hands off me." In case fans didn't jeer loudly enough, the valet would then step through the ropes and quickly spray the official's hands with the atomizer.

Once the bell rang, George was a typical wrestling bad guy, pulling hair and raking eyes when the referee wasn't looking. When the crowd jeered, George would look at the audience and sneer, "Peasants!" Victory generally was achieved when the Gorgeous One flipped his opponent to the canvas with a "flying side headlock"—a move that involved throwing his opponent to the mat while holding him in a headlock.

The routine worked so well that several fans attacked Gorgeous George. Once, a man put out his cigar on the back of the wrestler's calf. Other times, spectators grabbed George's expensive-looking ring robe (he said he owned 127), ripping it to shreds.

George's matches were televised in 50 different cities, and promoters all over North America wanted him to appear at their arenas. George was willing to accommodate them if he received one-third of the admission money—a demand few, if any, wrestlers have been able to make since.

"When George was hot, I never saw anything like it," said Lou Thesz. "He could sell out anywhere with anyone."

On at least two occasions, George promised to cut off his cherished curls if he lost. And, in both cases, fans got what they wanted. In 1962, George's head was shaved in center ring after a hair vs. mask match against the hooded Destroyer. Three years earlier, George lost his hair in Toronto to two-time National Wrestling Alliance (NWA) heavyweight champion Whipper Billy Watson.

Gorgeous George always made an elaborate entrance into the wrestling ring.

Gorgeous George in action

A rematch was scheduled, and this time, George pledged that his valet and his second wife, Cherie, would have their hair trimmed if Watson could beat him again. When Watson, a local hero, triumphed, Cherie tried running from the ring, but seven men held her down for the barber.

"Some women were crying for me," she remembered in *Whatever Happened to Gorgeous George?* "Others yelled it was what I deserved. People were grabbing for pieces of my hair. I was hysterical."

These types of antics enabled George to live the

life of a rich man. He purchased a turkey ranch, as well as a business called Gorgeous George's Ringside Bar, and drove four orchid-colored Cadillacs—to match the flowers he wore on his robes.

——— *George's Demise* ———

Gorgeous George had one serious problem. He was an alcoholic who, in Thesz's words, "went down the drain little by little." As the years passed, he seemed to be drunk more often than he was sober. Cherie divorced him. He ran out of money. He looked older than his years, choosing to spend his free time drinking rather than training in the gym.

Toward the end of his life, Gorgeous George's fellow wrestlers had a difficult time recognizing him in the dressing room. But once the camera went on and he held a microphone, he could still fascinate a crowd. Understanding this, promoters instructed the aging athlete to spend more time doing interviews and less time in the ring.

On Christmas Eve, 1963, when Gorgeous George was 48 years old, he suffered a heart attack in his Hollywood apartment. He died two days later. The Los Angeles City Council passed a resolution in memory of the showman who sold out the city's Olympic Auditorium 27 times. But the stripper that George had been dating was forced to borrow money from friends for the funeral.

The ceremony was the type of event the old wrestler would have loved. As both of George's ex-wives and his girlfriend cried, a group of wrestlers—including Baron Michel Leone and Indian chief Jules Strongbow—served as pallbearers. Ring announcer Jimmy Lennon sang hymns. Fans sent perfume and wreaths. Flowers smothered the orchid-colored coffin.

"If there had been a spark of life in old Gorgeous," said his old Houston friend Johnny James, "he would have stood up in that casket and taken a bow."

The Fabulous Moolah

4

Women's Wrestling

Occasionally, when promoters needed an extra gimmick to draw a crowd, they'd present a women's wrestling match, usually on a card headlined by men. In the United States, carnivals featured bouts between females since the early part of the twentieth century. Some performers, like Cora Livingstone, also wrestled both men and women in theaters during the vaudeville age. It was during the Great Depression that America's first well-known female wrestler, Mildred Burke, made her name.

———— *Mildred the Great* ————

Mildred Burke had been born Mildred Bliss in Kansas City, Missouri. She was attractive, athletic, and very strong, and she sometimes wondered whether she had been a great male wrestler in an earlier life. But perhaps the reason that she was so tough inside the ring was that her life outside the ring had been so difficult. She dropped out of school at age 15 and ended up working as a waitress on an Indian reservation in New Mexico. She was bored there and agreed to marry an old boyfriend and move with

Mildred Burke

Mildred gets rough with Mae Weston.

him to California. They had a hard time supporting themselves there and returned to Kansas City. The couple's troubles continued, and Mildred's husband walked out on her in 1932 when she was pregnant.

Throughout her pregnancy, Mildred worked as a waitress at her mother's diner, Mom's Café. One day she got into a conversation with Billy Wolfe, a wrestler who had been Missouri's middleweight champion. The idea of entering the profession excited her. After Mildred had her baby, Billy began helping her train.

In a gym above a garage, Mildred wrestled against a man who quickly scooped her off the mat, draped her body over his shoulders, and twirled her around in an "airplane spin." The move was supposed to make Mildred dizzy. But as she fell to the canvas, she managed to land on her feet, surprise her foe, and pin him.

Billy was impressed enough to take Mildred on the road to carnivals, changing her last name to Burke because he liked the way it sounded. Billy offered $25 to any man who could pin the female wrestler or force her to submit to an agonizing hold. In about 200 matches against men, Mildred only lost once. When that happened, she was battling a college wrestler in Omaha, Nebraska, and lifted him for a bodyslam. As he was about to fall, the man bent his knee, and it collided with Mildred's head. "The only time I was defeated, it wasn't because I was pinned," she said. "I got knocked out."

Mildred and Billy began making money on the carnival circuit and eventually married. But Mildred wanted matches against other women. Another female named Cora Jurgens had established a reputation as a tough competitor, and several matches were arranged to determine a women's world champion. Mildred hoped that these would be shoots, as she considered herself an athlete. But Jurgens's handlers apparently didn't want her popularity to decline if she lost. Once, they had Billy beaten up until he agreed to convince his wife to "do the job" for her foe. On another occasion, they reportedly paid the referee to rule in Jurgens's favor.

Mildred claimed that she was so angry after that match that she chased her opponent into the dressing room. There, Mildred supposedly pounded on her rival until Jurgens admitted that her opponent deserved the championship. Despite the results of the two matches, Billy billed his wife as the titleholder anyway, sending her around the country to appear on different promoters' shows. Mildred often slept in her car, traveling from one city to another. But she earned $50,000 in 1938—while the average major league baseball player made $6,000.

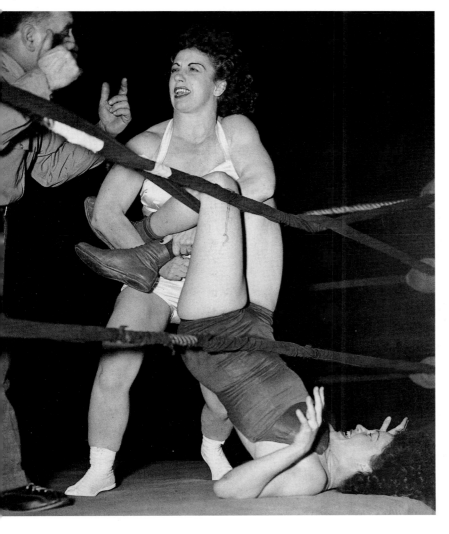

Mildred has her opponent on the ropes.

Meanwhile, her marriage was falling apart. Billy enjoyed collecting the money his wife earned but, beyond that, showed her little loyalty. He dated other female wrestlers behind his wife's back and was constantly looking for a younger woman to replace Mildred as champion. Sometimes, he'd ask one of her opponents to turn a match into a shoot when it was supposed to be a work. But Mildred was legitimately a good wrestler and always managed to defeat these challengers.

Eventually, Mildred fell in love with another man. He happened to be Billy's son from a previous marriage—G. Bill Wolfe. When Billy found out, he convinced his son to turn against Mildred. Then, both father and son beat her up.

Regardless of how much she suffered, Mildred would never give up her belt. In 1954, she took on June Byers, the woman both Wolfes hoped would take Mildred's place. The match was a shoot and, in the midst of it, Mildred's knee popped out of its socket. But she pushed it back and wrestled for a total of 47 minutes. Finally, the referee stopped the bout and awarded the championship to Byers, a move Mildred called a fraud.

Eventually, Byers married G. Bill Wolfe. After Mildred and Billy divorced, he married another one of her opponents, Nell Stewart.

The Fabulous Moolah

Lillian Ellison was a fellow female wrestler who was well aware of the tension between Mildred and her husband. A native of Columbia, South Carolina, she had been trained by Billy and her ex-husband, Johnny Long, in the late 1940s. But rather than depend on Wolfe to book her matches, Lillian traveled to New York to work for promoter Jack Pfefer. "Why do you want to wrestle?" Pfefer asked her. Lillian answered that her motive was the "moolah," or the money. Pfefer promptly renamed her Moolah.

Lillian was then one of the prettiest women in professional wrestling. She was part Irish and part

Lillian Ellison

Cherokee, with high cheekbones and long dark hair. At first, she played the role of a valet named Slave Girl Moolah, accompanying future heavyweight champion Buddy "Nature Boy" Rogers and a grappler called the Elephant Boy to the ring. Then, in 1956, she participated in a "Wrestle-Royal" in Baltimore. Thirteen women entered the match. After 11 were eliminated, Moolah disposed of Judy Grable to become the new women's champion.

For 29 years, Moolah held the belt, beating Donna Christiantello, Toni Rose, Penny Banner, and Sandy Parker, among other contenders. As Moolah aged, she became a heel, wearing sparkling glasses shaped like dollar signs and strutting around the ring with her arm behind her head like a beauty queen.

In addition to wrestling, Moolah trained such female stars as Lelani Kai, Judy Martin, and Wenona Little Heart. In fact, when Moolah lost her title in 1984, it was to another former student, Wendi Richter. A year later, Moolah won back the championship as the black-hooded Spider Lady, unmasking after the victory. She lost the title again but won it back another time before Sensational Sherri Martel captured the championship in 1987.

For a short period in the 1980s, a collection of women worked for an organization called GLOW, Gorgeous Ladies of Wrestling. But, generally, female wrestlers in the United States have appeared on cards dominated by men. Occasionally, one woman wrestler captures the public's attention, becoming as well known as some of the top male stars. In 1999, WWF champion Sable played that role, modeling for several magazine covers.

Incredibly, the Fabulous Moolah was still wrestling at that time. She even won the WWF title after Sable left that organization. "Everybody's worried about how old Moolah is," she said. "Well, I'll tell you this. When I retire, I'll be 100 years old. And I have a long way to go."

Moolah—still Fabulous

The Age of Territories

In 1948, St. Louis wrestling promoter Sam Muchnick called a meeting of his peers at the President Hotel in Waterloo, Iowa. Tony Stecher of Minneapolis, Minnesota; Al Haft of Columbus, Ohio; Max Clayton of Omaha, Nebraska; Pinky George of Des Moines, Iowa, and Orville Brown of Kansas City, Missouri, were there. Muchnick had a problem. He was competing against a promotion in his hometown run by Lou Thesz, the man who had won his first heavyweight championship nine years before, at age 21. Muchnick needed to offer the fans something that Thesz couldn't give them.

Each promoter had access to top wrestlers. The promoters promised to send their stars to each other's big shows, coming to the rescue if a competitor threatened any member of the group. They also agreed not to invade one another's territories. In other words, Haft would not promote a card in St. Louis because it belonged to Muchnick. And everyone accepted Des Moines as Pinky George's city. Furthermore, if any wrestler gave a particular promoter trouble, the entire group agreed not to book him. They would "blacklist" him from appearances until he changed his attitude.

Opposite page: Lou Thesz at the height of his popularity

Wrestling in Europe

While pro wrestling was thriving in the United States, fans in Europe enjoyed a different style of "mat wars." In England, Germany, and Austria, matches were fought in rounds. From 1960s through the early 1980s, British stars included Mick McManus, Giant Haystacks, Tony St. Clair, and Shirley "Big Daddy" Crabtree, pictured at right. Among the wrestlers seen on cards in Austria and Germany were Hansi Rooks, Wolfgang Saturski, Rene Lasartesse, and Stephan Wright.

In August 1982, Otto Wanz—a promoter based in Graz, Austria, and the number one babyface of the Catch Wrestling Association (CWA)—won the AWA championship from Nick Bockwinkel in St. Paul, Minnesota. Wanz lost the title to Bockwinkel in Chicago in October, but the win allowed the promoter to bill himself as a world champion.

Although European-style wrestling still existed in the late 1990s, both the WWF and WCW were televised around the continent and had toured Europe. As a result, the majority of European fans prefer the American brand of wrestling.

The six promoters pledged to recognize, and share, one heavyweight champion. Each man would run a separate territory with its own assortment of wrestlers, feuds, and story lines. But when the champion came to town, he would be billed as the most important man in wrestling. Fans would pack the arena to see the titlist defend his belt against the local hero. With this understanding, the National Wrestling Alliance (NWA) was born.

——— *The Birth of the NWA* ———

The NWA named Orville Brown as its first champion. With the titlist and stars like Buddy Rogers, available to everyone in the organization, other promoters soon signed up with the NWA. In St. Louis, Thesz grew weary of competing with Muchnick and offered to become his partner. Muchnick was thrilled and began pressuring the rest of the NWA to crown the young Hungarian champion.

A match was booked between Thesz and Brown. However, on November 1, 1949, the champion and another wrestler, Bob Bruns, were severely injured in an automobile accident. Later that month, the NWA announced that Thesz was its new kingpin. NWA officials also claimed that his belt was directly linked to the title Frank Gotch had won from George Hackenschmidt in 1908.

Except for an eight-month period in 1956, Thesz would hold the NWA championship for the next eight years. In the future, other NWA champions—such as Dick Hutton, Pat O'Connor, Dory Funk Jr., and Jack Brisco—would be patterned after Thesz. The titlist was a performer without gimmicks, a pure wrestler well versed in amateur holds. He also happened to be an exceptional shooter—a man who could win if a contender tried stealing the belt by luring him into a real fight.

Muchnick became the most powerful promoter in North America. Eventually, there were almost 40 NWA territories, with the title being defended as far away as Japan, Australia, and New Zealand.

Jack Brisco

Each year, the promoters met to decide whether to renew the champion's reign or pass the belt to someone else. Just to make sure that a titlist would be willing to do the job, or lose, when the time was right, the champion was required to post a bond of several thousand dollars. The money wasn't returned until the champion lost to the wrestler the promoters chose.

Not all wrestlers entered a territory with an attention-getting reputation. Some men were fine athletes but poor speakers. Others didn't have a gimmick catchy enough to attract attention. Because of this, managers became a crucial part of professional wrestling. When a wrestler arrived, the manager would do the talking, selling the grappler's talents to the public. Some managers stayed in one territory, joining forces with new heels who appeared to battle the local hero. Others traveled with specific wrestlers from region to region.

Sam Muchnick

— *The NWA Faces Competition* —

Even when the NWA was at its peak, there were always other leagues.

In a 1957 title defense in Chicago against The Flying Frenchman Edouard Carpentier, Thesz allegedly suffered a back injury. When the third fall of this two-out-of-three-fall match began, Thesz said he could not continue. Although the ring announcer proclaimed that Carpentier was the new champion, the NWA continued to recognize Thesz. But a group of midwestern promoters splintered away from the NWA, promoting the Frenchman as the titlist. Eventually, former amateur sensation Verne Gagne won the belt. In 1960, he issued a challenge to then-NWA champion Pat O'Connor. When he received no response, Gagne declared himself kingpin of the new American Wrestling Association (AWA), a Minneapolis-based outfit that he, not so coincidentally, owned.

On June 30, 1961, Nature Boy Buddy Rogers defeated O'Connor in front of 38,000 fans at

Buddy "Nature Boy"
Rogers early in his
career

Chicago's Comiskey Park. Rogers's appearances
were booked not through Muchnick or others in his
NWA inner circle, but through northeastern promoters Toots Mondt and Vince McMahon Sr. With
his swept-back blond hair, graceful moves in the
ring, and arrogant strut, Rogers was incredibly popular in Boston, New York, Philadelphia, and

Bruno Sammartino, left, and Buddy Rogers pose before their bout in Madison Square Garden. WWWF president Willie Gilzenberg is in the center.

Washington, D. C.—all cities controlled by Mondt and McMahon. But other promoters complained that he was rarely made available for weekend dates in their towns.

On January 24, 1963, Thesz defeated Rogers in a one-fall match in Toronto. The NWA announced that Thesz was the champion again. But Mondt and McMahon insisted that NWA rules specified that titles could only change hands in two-out-of-three-fall contests. Refusing to acknowledge the loss to Thesz, they presented Rogers as champion of their new World Wide Wrestling Federation (WWWF). In 1979, the name of this league would be shortened to the World Wrestling Federation (WWF).

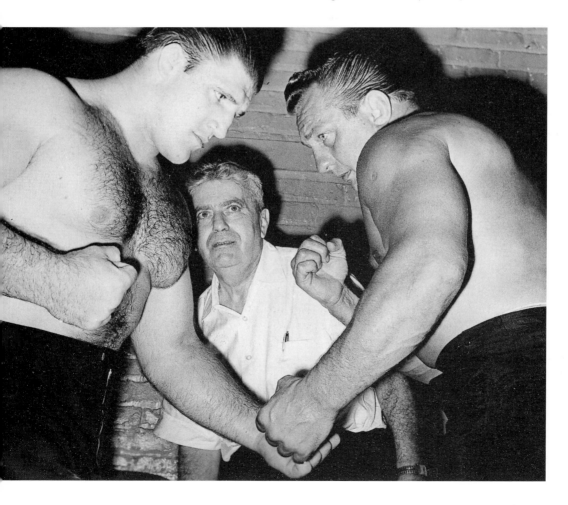

Bruno Sammartino

Rogers didn't hold his belt for long. On May 17, 1963, he faced Italian strongman Bruno Sammartino at Madison Square Garden. Within 48 seconds, Sammartino won the title. Some refer to this bout as the "official" beginning of the WWF.

There were now three separate world champions—one each for the NWA, AWA, and WWWF—and dozens of territories in North America. But there were also enough fans to keep nearly everyone in business. Each territory began to write its own history, with fans recalling powerful plot twists for years to come.

Rock 'n' Wrestling

In the early 1980s, a third generation promoter named Vincent Kennedy McMahon decided to branch out of his family's territory in the northeastern United States and conquer all of North America.

McMahon was the grandson of Roderick "Jess" McMahon, who had copromoted the Jess Willard vs. Jack Johnson championship boxing match in 1915. Jess operated out of New York's famed Madison Square Garden and eventually presented wrestling in addition to boxing shows. His son, Vincent James McMahon—also known as Vince Sr.—formed the organization that became the World Wrestling Federation.

Vincent Kennedy McMahon, or Vince Jr., was born in Pinehurst, North Carolina, in 1945 and, for the first few years of his life, didn't know his father. The boy and his mother were poor and lived in an 8-foot wide trailer. Vince suffered from both dyslexia and attention deficit disorder and got into trouble in school. His mother was married five times, and one of her husbands, an electrician, seemed to get a thrill out of beating the boy with wire and tools such as a screwdriver and a pipe wrench.

Opposite page: Hulk Hogan holds an action figure that was named after him.

"I think I would have been successful no matter what my chosen endeavor would have been," McMahon said, "but it could just as easily have been on this side of the law as that side of the law. And that's why I don't throw stones at anyone hardly for anything, with the exception of people who use their hardships growing up as a crutch, as an excuse for their behavior."

Vince Jr. was 12 years old when Vince Sr.'s wife, Juanita, set up a meeting between her husband and his son. "I immediately fell in love with him," the younger McMahon recalled. "I wanted to be just like him."

That included working in the wrestling business. As McMahon Jr. remembers: "The summer of '59, I was 14 years old, and my favorite wrestler was naturally a villainous type, Dr. Jerry Graham. He had [bleached blond] hair, and wore a red, riverboat gambler-type shirt. He had a 1959 blood-red Cadillac convertible . . . And I just thought he was the coolest guy."

Influenced by his idol, the teenager dyed his hair blond and began working out and dressing in the same blaring colors as Jerry Graham. Vince Sr. was not pleased. He urged his son to find a career separate from the wrestling profession. For a while Vince Jr. followed his father's advice. He attended military school and East Carolina University, then worked as a laborer and sold paper cups and adding machines. But none of these jobs made him happy. He pleaded with his father until Vince Sr. finally allowed him to enter the family business in 1971.

—— *Revolutionizing the WWF* ——

Vince Jr. examined the way wrestling was promoted on television, and he began making changes. Wrestlers began to tape interviews for specific cities, which were then inserted between matches on World Wide Wrestling Federation programs. Fans in Hartford, Connecticut, would see one interview, while viewers in Boston saw another. The new

Vince McMahon Jr. revolutionized his father's wrestling organization.

touch made the at-home viewers feel that the show had been made just for their hometown.

Vince Jr. also became the group's television announcer and altered the way the programs were produced. He added slow motion and other effects seen on regular sports programs. "You certainly don't have to be a genius to be able to use what everybody else is doing and apply it to your environment," McMahon said.

By 1980—after the World Wide Wrestling Federation had shortened its name to the World Wrestling Federation—the territory "was making more money than it had ever made, and so my dad was thinking it can't get any better than this," McMahon said. "And he was looking to get out."

Fearing that his father, who headed the WWF, would sell to somebody else, Vince Jr. purchased the organization in 1982. From the beginning, his goal was to turn the WWF into a national force. "I wish the regional system still existed," he said in 1999. "It would really be nice. But in order to do what I wanted to do, I had to have a national forum, in order to bring national advertisers to the World Wrestling Federation."

He used cable television, which was starting to be installed around the country, to accomplish this goal. McMahon created a program called All-American Wrestling on the USA cable network that featured the nation's best wrestlers. Other promoters were happy to send him tapes of their top talent, convinced that exposure on the national station would help business. What the promoters didn't realize was that McMahon was planning to lure these wrestlers to the WWF and wanted the public to be familiar with them.

The fact that Vince Sr. and the other promoters had gentlemen's agreements to stay out of each other's territories didn't matter. Vince Jr. could not be stopped. He started paying television stations in different cities to run his programs opposite wrestling shows that had been televised locally for decades. Other promoters contacted Vince Sr., complaining that his son was going to put them out of business. "My dad's phone started ringing, but he didn't have any control then," McMahon said. "He was working for me."

The World Wrestling Federation, which already had a roster of superstars like Andre the Giant and Jimmy "Superfly" Snuka, offered the best wrestlers from different parts of North America lucrative deals to join. Territories were suddenly operating without their top talent, and the WWF would visit these places, putting on shows with the wrestlers who had just departed.

Rowdy Roddy Piper, the best heel on the continent, arrived in the WWF from the Carolinas. The Junkyard Dog, the most popular African-American babyface, came from Oklahoma's Mid-South territory. Former NWA tag team champions Jack and Jerry Brisco sold their percentage of a wrestling promotion in Georgia. Even Mean Gene Okerlund, a wisecracking announcer from Minneapolis, switched sides. McMahon's most valuable addition was Terry Gene Bollea, a former bass player from Tampa, Florida, who called himself Hulk Hogan.

Jimmy "Superfly" Snuka

LeRoy Brown, left, gets pulled apart by the Junkyard Dog.

The Incredible Hulk

What made Hogan different from other performers was the fact that people outside of wrestling already knew him. In 1982, he'd played a character called "Thunderlips" in the boxing movie *Rocky III*. After the movie was released, Hogan appeared on talk shows and charmed audiences with his quick, articulate answers and sense of humor. With his blond hair, Fu Manchu mustache, bronzed skin, and large, muscular body—6-foot-9 and 330 pounds—the Hulkster shined on television. McMahon saw him as a crossover celebrity, the type of entertainer who fans and non-fans alike could appreciate.

Terry Bollea was born on August 11, 1953, and attended Robinson High School in Tampa. After graduation, he attended the University of South Florida for several semesters. Bollea gained a reputation as an incredibly strong weight lifter in local gyms, a tough barroom bouncer, and a bass player in local bands—combining the mixture of muscle and rock 'n' roll that McMahon would treasure.

Bollea was a huge wrestling fan and frequently attended matches in his area, paying particular attention to former World Wide Wrestling Federation champion Superstar Billy Graham. With bleached blond hair, a muscular physique, and an incredible ability to do interviews, Graham became Bollea's role model.

After being trained in Tampa by former Japanese wrestler Hiro Hatsuda, Bollea made his debut as Terry "the Hulk" Boulder in small territories around the southern United States. His weightlifting buddy from Tampa, Ed Leslie, was billed as his brother, Eddie Boulder.

In Georgia, Bollea was given the name Sterling Golden. Then, in 1979, Vince McMahon Sr. brought him to the WWF as the Incredible Hulk Hogan. With white-haired, trash-talking Freddie Blassie as his manager, Hogan played the part of a monster

Terry "the Hulk" Boulder, left, and Ed Leslie strike a pose.

Andre the Giant

Perhaps Hogan's most famous opponent was Andre the Giant, another wrestler whose reputation extended beyond the ring.

Andre, who was listed as 7-foot-4 and more than 500 pounds, was afflicted with acromegaly, a disease sometimes called giantism. The disorder produces an excessive secretion of growth hormones, causing a gradual enlargement of the head, face, hands, feet, and chest.

The giant—born Andre Rene Rousimoff in Grenoble, France, in 1946—grew up hoping to become a schoolteacher. But he was teased as a teenager and yearned to escape to a place where people would accept him. "I hated not being like everybody else," he said.

In 1966, Montreal wrestler Frank Valois discovered him during a European tour. In 1970—after training for professional wrestling—Andre toured Japan as Monster Rousimoff. The next year, he moved to Montreal, where he was billed as Jean Ferre, a happy giant who only used his superhuman power when provoked. In 1973, Valois—who had become Andre's best friend—set up a meeting with Vince McMahon Sr., who renamed him Andre the Giant.

McMahon Sr. made Andre one of the World Wide Wrestling Federation's top stars but also helped out other promoters by booking him on big cards in their territories. Andre was constantly on the road, since almost every promoter wanted him.

At first, Andre was quite athletic. He could leave his feet and deliver a flying dropkick or lift an opponent and fall backward with him to the mat, arching his neck to execute a perfect "German suplex." Because of his size, he was believed to be one of wrestling's strongest men. He even considered trying out for football's Washington Redskins. But acromegaly is a condition that worsens over time. He began to slow down in the ring and suffered from back problems. Yet, even when he had to wear a back brace under his wrestling tights, Andre wouldn't quit. The wrestling arena was where he was most comfortable.

In January 1993, 46-year-old Andre went to France to visit his sick father. A few days later, his father died. Andre attended the funeral, then decided to remain in France to spend time with relatives. On January 27, he went to sleep in his hotel room and died of an apparent heart attack.

heel, an enormous bad guy causing turmoil in a territory. After squashing one opponent after another—and intriguing wrestling audiences—Hogan faced off against Andre the Giant, billed as 7-foot-4 and more than 500 pounds, in a battle of mammoths.

The feud started when Hogan used an elbow pad supposedly loaded with some type of weapon to attack Andre on television. Then, to the astonishment of spectators, Hogan lifted and bodyslammed the Giant. On August 9, 1980, the two met again at Shea Stadium, the home of baseball's New York Mets. Even though Andre won, the fact that Hogan was able to lift and slam his foe established the villain as one of the strongest men in wrestling.

The same year, Hogan toured Japan for the first time, and immediately caught fire in the Asian country. He recorded an album of rock 'n' roll songs, and Hulk Hogan dolls and comics were released. Although Hogan would gain his biggest fame in the WWF, "Hulkamania" was born in Japan.

In 1981, Hogan moved to the Minneapolis-based American Wrestling Association (AWA). There, wisecracking Johnny Valiant managed him and marketed him as a heel. However, fans loved watching the charismatic wrestler and cheered him. As a result, the AWA eliminated Valiant and turned Hogan into a babyface. For years, the AWA had been built around more traditional wrestlers, with amateur backgrounds. But Hogan was the organization's most popular draw ever and the number one attraction in professional wrestling.

Andre the Giant vs. Hulk Hogan was a popular matchup.

According to one story, AWA promoter Verne Gagne—an amateur great in the 1940s—once challenged Hogan to a shoot in the dressing room, claiming that the new sensation's lack of knowledge about pure wrestling would handicap him. Hogan is said to have accepted the dare and, with the other wrestlers watching, muscled the aging Gagne down to the floor before mercifully releasing him. Whether the incident actually occurred, the wrestlers who told this tale were trying to convey that the days of promoting men who viewed themselves as pure wrestlers were over. The movement that Vince McMahon Jr. would call "sports entertainment" was starting.

Hogan wanted Gagne to make him the AWA world champion, but Gagne refused. Among other reasons, Gagne reportedly thought that Hogan was too large to hold the title. Many promoters at the time believed that a smaller man defending his belt against one giant after another was more dramatic. In November 1983, while he was touring Japan again, Hogan had a meeting with Vince McMahon Sr. He promised Hogan the WWF title and more money than Gagne was paying him. Hogan sent the AWA a telegram from Japan, informing the office that he was quitting.

On December 26, 1983, Bob Backlund, the pure wrestler who had held the WWF championship since 1978, unexpectedly lost the title to the Iron Sheik, an Iranian heel, in Madison Square Garden. Backlund was trapped in the Sheik's camel clutch— a move where a wrestler crouches behind his foe, places his hands under his opponent's chin, and bends him backward—when his manager, Arnold Skaaland, threw in a white towel, surrendering the match. A month later, Hogan blazed into the same building, pummeled the Sheik, bounced off the ropes, leaped into the air, lowered a leg across the Iranian's neck, and pinned him. The Hulk Hogan era had begun, and professional wrestling's territory system was ending.

Rockin' the Boat

Vince McMahon Sr. didn't live long enough to see his son carry out his dreams. By the time the elder McMahon died in 1984, Vince Jr. had started the rock 'n' wrestling connection, attracting attention by using popular entertainers in the WWF story lines. "We are, in fact, like the early days of rock 'n' roll," the younger McMahon said, "in that we're a little bit naughty, and we like to be."

The rock 'n' wrestling connection began when singer Cyndi Lauper appeared on a WWF program with manager Captain Lou Albano, who had been featured in her hit video, *Girls Just Want To Have Fun*. Everything was going well until Albano—a gruff, bearded man with rubber bands hanging from the hoops piercing his face—began belittling women. Lauper smacked Albano and vowed to prove that she was a better manager. On July 23, 1984, she managed Wendi Richter in a match against the Fabulous Moolah, the women's champion since 1956. Albano was in Moolah's corner. When Richter won and Lauper climbed into the ring to celebrate, photos of the pair ran in newspapers all over the world.

Wrestling was "in." Celebrities flocked to Madison Square Garden to watch the WWF. On February 18, 1985, MTV, the music cable television network, broadcast a match between Hogan and Rowdy Roddy Piper. Not only did Cyndi Lauper get involved in the action, but Mr. T—the rugged actor who had appeared with Hogan in *Rocky III* and who was currently the star of the popular TV show, *The A-Team*—stormed the ring. McMahon soon announced that if people wanted to actually see Mr. T wrestle, they could watch "WrestleMania" on March 31. The highlight of the extravaganza would

Wendi Richter captured the women's title from the Fabulous Moolah in 1984.

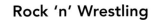
*Hulk Hogan and
Mr. T headlined
"WrestleMania."*

be Hogan and Mr. T against Piper and Paul "Mr. Wonderful" Orndorff.

"WrestleMania" would become a yearly spectacular for the WWF. Hogan and Mr. T appeared on David Letterman's late-night talk show and hosted the comedy program, *Saturday Night Live,* to increase interest. Fans all over the country were told that they could watch a live transmission of "WrestleMania" on closed circuit television at local movie theaters and arenas or on pay-per-view, a brand new option to people with cable television. To everyone's surprise, pay-per-view orders poured in, making the WWF a leader in this field.

The card was everything the WWF had promised. Boxing great Muhammad Ali was a guest referee.

Mr. T spins his opponent as his partner, Hulk Hogan, cheers him on.

Former New York Yankee baseball manager Billy Martin was a special ring announcer. Liberace—a piano player known for his massive diamond rings, full-length fur coats, and candelabras—danced in the ring with Rockefeller Center's famous Rockettes. Mr. T delighted viewers by actually wrestling, lifting up Piper and twirling him in the "airplane spin" at one point. The main event ended when Hogan pinned Orndorff. Apparently angry about the loss, Piper turned against his partner, making Orndorff a babyface and keeping spectators interested in the WWF storylines.

With the group's appeal proven, NBC started showing WWF matches as regular Saturday night specials—the first time network television had featured professional wrestling since the days of Gorgeous George. "WrestleMania" also continued to attract an audience, year after year. In 1987, lovable Andre the Giant turned heel and demanded a shot at Hogan's title. The WWF pretended that the 1980 feud between these superstars never existed and told millions of new fans that these wrestlers would be meeting for the first time at "WrestleMania III." On March 29, 1987, Hogan defeated Andre in Michigan's Pontiac Silverdome. According to the WWF, 93,173 fans, paying about $1.6 million, were inside the football stadium, more than doubling past records. On pay-per-view alone, the WWF took in $10.3 million.

One by one, most of the old territories died. But McMahon had even more changes in mind. For years, he'd resented the fact that he had to pay state athletic commissions to regulate his wrestling matches. So, at a 1989 hearing in front of New Jersey politicians, WWF officials revealed the secret that promoters had always feared would kill the business. Athletic commissions weren't needed, the WWF said, because professional wrestling wasn't a sport. The winners and losers were determined beforehand, and wrestlers worked hard not to hurt each other.

"We're storytellers," McMahon would say later. "This is a soap opera performed by the greatest actors and athletes in the world."

Former World Wide Wrestling Federation champion Bruno Sammartino wasn't alone when he grumbled, "McMahon made wrestling trash."

But in 1989 McMahon paid little attention to the criticism. In the months after the admission that wrestling was sports entertainment, the company enjoyed its best business ever.

7

THE FIGHT FOR POWER

While the World Wrestling Federation was swallowing up much of the United States, other promoters made several attempts to band together to fight their common enemy. In 1984, the NWA returned to the New York City area—the heart of the WWF's territory—for the first time in more than 20 years. At New Jersey's Meadowlands, wrestlers based in North Carolina, Georgia, and Puerto Rico showcased their skills, hoping to lure away the WWF's growing audience. Later the same year, a group calling itself Pro Wrestling USA appeared on television in New York, featuring performers from both the NWA and AWA. Pro Wrestling USA stars also included wrestlers who had recently been headliners in the WWF, including former champion Bob Backlund and Sergeant Slaughter, an extremely popular athlete who played the role of a flag-waving Marine.

The promoters were trying to show the wrestling public that, united, they could be more powerful than McMahon. But, behind the scenes, there were many divisions. McMahon joked that after his rivals agreed that they wanted to put him out of business, they couldn't even decide what to order for lunch.

Opposite page: Sergeant Slaughter appealed to the patriotism of fans in the 1980s.

Still, the efforts continued. In 1986, wrestlers from eight different territories participated in an all-day tournament at the Superdome in New Orleans. At the end of the seven-and-a-half hour show, the Road Warriors—sneering, muscular tag team partners known for their partially shaved heads, painted faces, and indestructible appearance—won the Jim Crockett Sr. Memorial Cup, beating Ron Garvin and Magnum T. A. in the finals. The prize was named after the late North Carolina promoter, whose son, Jim Crockett Jr., had helped organize the event.

But Crockett's allies suspected that, like McMahon, he had designs of taking over professional wrestling. This was confirmed when Crockett held his own shows in Memphis and Florida without cooperating with the promoters in those territories. Eventually, he purchased the leagues based in Oklahoma and Kansas City, and, like McMahon, started promoting all over the United States.

Crockett understood the tastes of more traditional fans, who thought of the WWF as a "cartoon show." The matches on Crockett's cards often seemed more like wrestling and less like entertainment. In addition, Crockett controlled the bookings of the NWA champion and could prevent him from appearing on shows in other territories.

This alone would have given Crockett an enormous advantage over other promoters. But Crockett was also fortunate to have one of wrestling's true legends as an NWA champion. Ric Flair, who held the belt for most of the 1980s, was an extraordinary athlete well-versed in crowd psychology. He controlled the moods of his audience, getting them to boo, cheer, and scream when he wanted. Against a lesser performer, Flair would throw himself around the ring and make his opponent look like a superman. And, he could ignite an arena before a match even began by removing his sequin robe and dramatically strutting. In interviews, he'd been compared to Gorgeous George.

"What's the difference between Flair and everybody else in this dressing room?" future WWF and WCW heavyweight champion Randy "Macho Man"

Savage asked a group of wrestlers early in his career. "Everybody else is in black and white, and Ric Flair's in living color."

Both Flair's peers and fans echoed Savage's observation. Most agreed that he was the greatest professional wrestler of his generation.

—— *Showing Some Flair* ——

Richard Morgan Fliehr was born February 25, 1949, in a suburb of Minneapolis. As the only child of a gynecologist who also worked as a local theater director, Flair was adored by his parents. While other entertainers invented deprived backgrounds to better relate to their audience, the champion

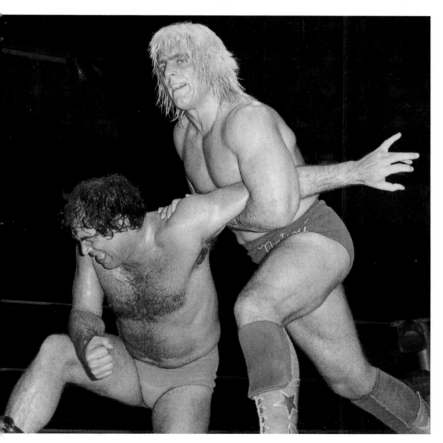

Ric Flair

Pro Wrestling

Ric Flair called himself "Nature Boy" after the legendary Buddy Rogers.

bragged about being a child of privilege who still led the good life. "I'm a Rolex-wearing, limousine-riding, Leer jet-flying son of a gun," he'd shout during interviews, "custom made from head to toe."

From his earliest years, Flair's athletic skills were obvious. He was the high school heavyweight wrestling champion of the state of Minnesota and played offensive guard on the University of Minnesota football team. But Flair's poor grades prevented him from remaining on the team during his sophomore year. Frustrated, he dropped out of school and began thinking of other opportunities. His friend Greg Gagne—son of AWA owner Verne Gagne—suggested that Ric attend the organization's pro wrestling camp. Flair began training with Gagne, quit, then returned a year later. On December 10, 1972, Flair began his wrestling career, going to a 10-minute draw with George "Scrap Iron" Gadaski.

As he learned the profession, Flair largely worked as a jobber in the AWA, losing to more established wrestlers. But Flair caught the attention of Wahoo

McDaniel, a popular American Indian wrestler who had played professional football. McDaniel told Jim Crockett about the young man's skills, and the promoter brought Flair to the Carolinas in 1974.

Bleaching his long hair blond, Flair began to develop his character. He used the figure four leglock—a move where a wrestler tangles his legs around his opponent—as a finisher. He called himself the Nature Boy, like another cocky blond, former NWA and WWWF champion Nature Boy Buddy Rogers. But after winning several regional titles, Flair's career nearly ended. On October 4, 1975, he was flying to a match in a Cessna 310 aircraft when the plane crashed in Wilmington, North Carolina. The pilot died. Wrestlers Johnny Valentine and Bob Bruggers suffered partial paralysis. Another wrestler, Tim "Mr. Wrestling" Woods, and promoter David Crockett—Jim's brother—came away with minor injuries. Flair's back was broken in three places.

But, in less than a year, he was back in the squared circle, his movements as quick as ever. The only evidence of the accident was a knot under Flair's skin, a calcium deposit inserted by doctors to strengthen his back. Working as a heel, he feuded with Woods—who had also recovered from the crash—Bobo Brazil, and Rick Steamboat. In 1979, he beat the original Nature Boy Buddy Rogers with the figure four leglock, earning the right to mimic the legend's gestures and wrestling maneuvers.

On September 17, 1981, Flair became the NWA heavyweight champion for the first time, defeating the American Dream, Dusty Rhodes, in Kansas City. For the next two years, Flair defended the belt in every territory, going against the local hero and generally just escaping with the title.

Sometimes, the finish of the match was what wrestlers call a "Broadway." The babyface would have Ric tied up for the pin when the bell rang. The fans would erupt, thinking that the championship changed hands—until the ring announcer told the crowd that the time limit had expired before the referee's hand could slap the mat for the third time.

Dusty Rhodes was known as "the American Dream."

Ric Flair manhandles Paul "Mr. Wonderful" Orndorff.

On other occasions, Flair was tossed over the ropes in the course of a brawl. When he returned to the ring, the babyface pinned him. But before Flair's opponent was awarded the belt, the audience would be informed that NWA rules prohibited throwing a man over the top rope. The babyface was disqualified, and Flair was still the champion.

Both finishes allowed the local hero to maintain his status as the biggest star in the territory and claim that if it weren't for the NWA rules, he'd have beaten Flair. And when Flair returned, the fans were just as excited as during his previous visit. This time, they were sure that they'd witness a historic title change.

Over the next few years, other men would also hold the NWA championship, including Harley

Race, Kerry Von Erich, and Rhodes. But it was Flair who always won the belt back and symbolized the NWA. His interviews were unforgettable. He called himself Space Mountain and warned opponents, "To be the man, you have to beat the man." Before walking off camera, he'd throw back his hair and shout, "Wooooo!"

Jim Crockett could not run a big card without Flair in the main event. In 1985—the same year as "WrestleMania I"—30,000 spectators packed the minor league baseball stadium in Charlotte, North Carolina, to watch Flair against Nikita Koloff at the first "Great American Bash." Four months later, fans paid an amazing $936,000 to see Flair and Rhodes battle at the third annual "Starcade." Soon, both "Starcade" and the "Great American Bash" would become yearly pay-per-view events for the company. And NWA fans would insist that, in a shoot, Flair would have no problem destroying Hulk Hogan.

"To be the man, you have to beat the man."

— The Pay-Per-View Tug of War —

Crockett first tried getting into the pay-per-view business on Thanksgiving in 1987. The fourth annual "Starcade" card featured Ric Flair as challenger against Ron Garvin, who had won the NWA title in September. Crockett had recently purchased the Mid-South territory, based in Oklahoma, and had unlimited access to the best wrestlers from that region, including Sting, Rick Steiner, Hot Stuff Eddie Gilbert, and Steve "Dr. Death" Williams. The event was to be held in Chicago, a bigger city than the places normally associated with Crockett's territory.

Up until this time, the WWF had been the only promotion to take advantage of pay-per-view. McMahon tried to sidetrack the NWA's attempt to gain equality. On the same day as "Starcade," the WWF presented its first "Survivor Series." The rules were intriguing. Teams of five superstars each would enter the ring to do battle with one another. When one man was eliminated, he'd have to return to the dressing room, leaving his partners behind to

Randy "Macho Man" Savage

continue the fight. This allowed fans to see dramatic confrontations in which a wrestler might be battling two or three foes at once.

Learning of McMahon's plans for the evening pay-per-view show, Crockett planned to schedule "Starcade" in the late afternoon. Wrestling fans would then have the opportunity to watch two events in a row. Crockett was confident that, when viewers compared the products, the majority would believe that the NWA put on a better production.

But the WWF didn't want the competition. The organization sent a message to cable television companies that if they wanted the "Survivor Series," they could not show any other wrestling events 60 days before or 21 days after it. The motive was clearly to keep the NWA off of pay-per-view. Because the WWF's previous pay-per-view events had been so successful, the cable companies took the condition seriously. The majority ran only the "Survivor Series."

On January 24, 1988, the NWA ran another pay-per-view show. This time, it was available in more locations. But the WWF offered an alternative, presenting what it called its first "Royal Rumble" (in reality, this type of match had been held several months before at a St. Louis show that was not televised) on the USA cable television network. Twenty wrestlers participated in the bout. Viewers were told that earlier in the night each man had picked a number. Wrestlers one and two battled when the match began. But two minutes later, a bell rang, and wrestler number three joined the conflict. Two minutes after that, wrestler number four entered, and so on. The only way a participant could be eliminated from this free-for-all was by being thrown over the top rope to the arena floor.

In the years to come, the "Royal Rumble" would expand to include 30 wrestlers. Newcomers would rush the ring every 90 seconds, as opposed to two minutes. The event would also be offered on pay-per-view.

But in 1988, the fact that anyone with cable television could tune into the "Rumble" hurt the NWA's pay-per-view sales. Rather than back down from the pressure, the NWA ran a special—called "Clash of the Champions"—on the TBS cable station at the same time the WWF was presenting "WrestleMania IV" on pay-per-view on March 27, 1988. An estimated seven to eight million viewers—more than twice the number of people who watched "WrestleMania IV"—saw the "Clash." In the main event of the "Clash," Flair, once again the NWA champion, went to a 45-minute draw with Sting, a popular wrestler with spiked hair and swirling face paint. The card put a dent in the WWF's biggest show of the year and proved that the NWA was not going to surrender to its better-known opponent without a fight.

Sting

8

Japanese Pro Wrestling

While the WWF and NWA were at war, fans in Japan were busy following the competition between promotions in their country. For years, American professional wrestling had been influenced by events in Asia. Wrestlers returning from tours of Japan had brought back maneuvers from that nation—martial arts-inspired kicks, spectacular flying moves, and a more rugged, athletic style. It was in Japan that most of the big stars began using entrance music before their matches in the early 1970s, and promoters started selling the kinds of souvenirs and T-shirts later found at American arenas.

The Japanese also understood how to market to young people. In 1981, Tiger Mask, a high-flying, masked wrestler whose character was based on a popular comic strip, first appeared, drawing children to his matches. Seven years earlier, 16-year-old Mach Fumiake became the first of several female wrestling stars to record her songs, sparking the Japanese version of the rock 'n' wrestling connection.

Americans brought professional wrestling to Japan after World War II. In 1951, former boxing

Opposite page: Tiger Mask in full regalia

champion Joe Louis led a tour of boxers and wrestlers to Japan to entertain U. S. servicemen stationed there after American forces occupied the country at the end of the war. Within a month, several competitors from the Japanese sports of judo and sumo wrestling announced their plans to become professional wrestlers.

The Mighty Rikidozan

A man called Rikidozan ("Rugged Mountain Road"), who had retired from the ancient sport of sumo in 1950, was one who wished to become a professional wrestler. His real name was Kim Sin-Nak, and he'd been born in 1924 in what is now North Korea.

Rikidozan was the first great Japanese pro wrestler.

Because Koreans were often discriminated against in Japan, he took the Japanese name Mitsuhiro Momota and claimed to be a native of the Japanese city of Nagasaki. His true origins were not revealed until years after he died.

On October 28, 1951, Rikidozan had his first match, wrestling American Bobby Bruns to a 10-minute draw. The next year he moved to Hawaii, training at a wrestling gym while engaging in matches in both Honolulu and San Francisco. In 1953, he returned home, formed his own promotion and began importing American wrestlers to work as heels against the Japanese.

Few Japanese had television at this time, but a February 1954 tag team tournament featuring Rikidozan and partner Masahiko Kimura was carried on two networks. Thousands of people packed themselves in front of Tokyo store windows to watch the pair take on Americans Ben and Mike Sharpe. Soon, Panasonic became the first Japanese company to manufacture televisions. As this luxury became more affordable, Rikidozan established himself as one of Japan's first true television stars.

In December 1954, Rikidozan and Kimura met for the first Japanese heavyweight championship. Kimura later claimed that the match was supposed to be a work that would end in a draw. But he said that Rikidozan double-crossed him and began shooting, or trying to win the title.

In 1957, NWA champion Lou Thesz became the first American heavyweight titlist to defend his belt in Japan. Naturally, his opponent was Rikidozan. The two wrestled to a 30-minute draw in front of 30,000 fans.

In 1962, Rikidozan traveled to Los Angeles, where promoters had broken away from the NWA and formed a group called the World Wrestling Association (WWA). The Japanese star defeated Freddie Blassie to capture the organization's crown, becoming the first Asian to win an American "world championship."

Wrestling had become huge in Japan, and Rikidozan was a very wealthy man. He bought his own wrestling arena, along with nightclubs, apartment houses, hotels, and golf courses. The yakuza, or Japanese organized crime families, was also involved in these businesses. On occasion, the criminals found themselves in conflict with the stubborn wrestler. On December 8, 1963, a gangster followed Rikidozan into a restroom in a Tokyo nightclub and warned him not to interfere with the criminals' business interests. When Rikidozan responded with an insult, he was stabbed.

According to one account, the wrestler staggered back into the nightclub, grabbed the microphone, and cursed at his attacker while slowly dying. But the story is the type of exaggerated tale often heard in dressing rooms at wrestling arenas. Less sensational reports of the incident have Rikidozan being rushed to the hospital in an ambulance. He was told that his injury was not serious and would heal. A week later, though, the wound began bleeding again, and the 39-year-old father of Japanese professional wrestling died.

Investigations that followed the murder uncovered a great deal of yakuza influence in Japanese professional wrestling. Some arenas refused to allow their buildings to be used for the events. There was concern that wrestling would no longer interest the Japanese public. But Rikidozan had prepared for his eventual passing from the game. Two of the students at his dojo, or training academy, stepped in, displaying enough skill, charisma, and business savvy to carry Japanese wrestling through the 1990s.

Shohei Baba

—— *Baba and Inoki Take Over* ——

Shohei Baba, one of Rikidozan's students, was a former Japanese baseball pitcher. At 6-foot-9, he was taller than most of his countrymen, allowing American promoters to later bill him as 7-foot-3 Giant Baba. Although less muscular than most wrestlers, young Baba was a pure athlete who had the stamina to wrestle matches as long as 90 minutes.

No man in the history of professional wrestling has ever appeared in more consecutive bouts without taking time off for illness or injury. From 1960 to 1984, Baba wrestled in 3,764 straight matches. And that was only in Japan! If his matches in America are included, the number is closer to 4,100.

The other student was Kanji "Antonio" Inoki, whose family had moved from Japan to Brazil, where he became a high school champion in shot put and discus. Both Baba and Inoki made their professional debuts on September 30, 1960, at the old Daito Ku Gymnasium in Tokyo. Baba defeated Yonetaro Tanaka, and Inoki lost to Korean sensation Kintaro Oki. No one at the time realized that both Inoki and his opponent would later be elected senators in their respective countries. Over the next few months, Inoki and Baba wrestled each other several times, with Baba winning on every occasion. The two later became tag team partners, taking on the best teams America could send to the country. On October 31, 1967, the pair won the Japanese international tag team championship from Cowboy Bill Watts and Tarzan Tyler. Behind the scenes, the two were extremely competitive with one another, and, in 1972, each started rival wrestling promotions.

Baba's All-Japan Pro Wrestling was a traditional wrestling organization, emphasizing athletics over gimmicks. Baba established a relationship with the NWA, which frequently sent its champion to Japan for title defenses. On three separate occasions, Baba won the NWA title, beating Jack Brisco in 1974 and Harley Race in both 1979 and 1980. These victories occurred while the NWA champion was visiting Asia, and Baba always lost the belt before the tour ended.

As a promoter, Baba also gained a reputation as one of the most honest men in the business—so much so that wrestling's Living Legend Bruno Sammartino offered to wrestle for free if All-Japan ever experienced financial problems.

Inoki's New Japan Pro Wrestling was a flashier promotion. Inoki's goal was staging spectacular events to spotlight the group—and himself. In 1973,

Antonio Inoki

he defeated Johnny Powers for the National Wrestling Federation (NWF) title. Although the NWF was a small promotion, the victory gave Inoki the right to claim that he owned an American "world championship." Unfortunately, American fans were not as fascinated by Inoki as his countrymen were. When he defended the belt in the United States, attendance was poor.

In 1976, Inoki finally received the worldwide attention he craved when he challenged boxing champion Muhammad Ali to a boxer versus wrestler match in Tokyo. The legendary Ali agreed to the clash after being offered $6 million, more money than he'd ever received before for a single match. The pair worked hard to hype the match. Inoki knocked out Willem Ruska, a two-time Olympic gold medalist in judo, in a tune-up fight, beginning a New Japan trend of pitting wrestlers against champions from other fighting disciplines. Ali toured the United States with Freddie Blassie as his manager, delivering heel interviews for wrestling audiences. During an appearance at a World Wide Wrestling Federation show in Philadelphia, Ali interfered in one of babyface Gorilla Monsoon's matches. Monsoon received international publicity for scooping up the boxing great, draping him over his shoulders, and spinning him around before dumping him on the canvas.

Like the confrontation with Monsoon, the Inoki fight was supposed to be a work. Ali would use his boxing ability to bloody Inoki. When the referee attempted to check the cut, Inoki, the brave warrior, would insist on continuing the fight. Finally, Ali, the caring sportsman, would tell the official to stop the fight because he couldn't stand to inflict any more punishment. With the boxer distracted, Inoki would pounce, beating Ali with an enzuigiri—a move in which a wrestler leaps off the mat and kicks his leg in a crescent formation, zapping his opponent in the back of the head. While Ali would seem like a compassionate athlete, Inoki would receive acclaim for beating his famous opponent. With this win, he could sell out any arena in the United States.

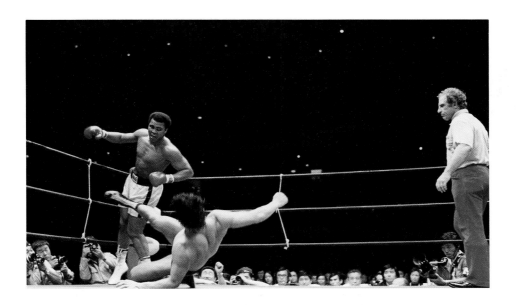

But Ali had second thoughts about taking part in the sham. After arriving in Japan, he nearly pulled out of the match. Finally, the two sides agreed to a shoot. Ali would wear his gloves and box. Inoki could not kick his opponent in the head or throat, punch him in the face with bare knuckles, execute a choke, or deliver a suplex—a move where a wrestler lifts his foe and falls backward, driving the man's back into the mat. With these restrictions, the bout was a bore. Inoki stayed on his back most of the match, out of range of Ali's punches, kicking at the boxer's legs. Although Ali was hospitalized from the constant blows, there was almost no action. After 15 rounds, the match ended in a draw, prompting fans in the arena, as well as at many American locations where the bout was shown, to riot.

Japan's wrestling business declined. But Inoki always had an angle. On August 26, 1979, he and Baba briefly put aside their differences to stage a card. In the main event, the two superstars teamed together for the first time in eight years, defeating the wild pair of Tiger Jeet Singh and Abdullah the Butcher.

Later that year, Inoki beat World Wrestling Federation champion Bob Backlund for the belt in

Heavyweight boxing champion Muhammad Ali took on Inoki in a match in Japan.

the city of Tokushima. A week later in Tokyo, Backlund was scheduled to win back the title before leaving Japan. But when Tiger Jeet Singh interfered in the outcome, Japanese officials announced that the match was a no contest, and Inoki was still champion. The WWF was furious about the ruling and never acknowledged the title change to American fans. Inoki saved face with his followers by vacating the championship because of the questionable nature of the finish.

Tiger Makes His Mark

The debut of Tiger Mask changed professional wrestling forever. At 5-foot-5 and 160 pounds, Sotoru Sayama was smaller than most Japanese wrestlers but determined to succeed. He spent two years wrestling in England and Mexico and became an expert in Mexico's aerial "lucha libre" style.

Tiger Mask delivers a flying dropkick while fighting Black Tiger.

When he returned to Japan in 1981, Sayama transformed himself into Tiger Mask. His costume, which included a mask decorated with tiger stripes and lined with white fur, intrigued children but the way he moved in the ring had the biggest impact. Tiger Mask dove through the ropes onto opponents standing on the arena floor. He frequently won his matches with a moonsault, flipping backward off the top rope onto a foe. He became such an attraction that both the NWA and WWF had him win their junior heavyweight titles. And wrestlers twice his size in Europe, Japan, and the United States began mimicking his moves.

Sayama was among a group of wrestlers who rejected the traditional American wrestling style for a more fluid, Japanese presentation. Over the next two decades, groups of these athletes would break away from the major Japanese promotions and start federations specializing in what they called "shoot-fighting" or hybrid wrestling. Acknowledging that fans understood the way the business operated, the promoters of these leagues claimed that their matches were actual shoots.

Because these men had an association with professional wrestling, fans remained suspicious of the claims. But many of the matches presented by the Pancrase and Rings promotions in the 1990s appeared to be legitimate. The wrestlers tended to be thin and muscular, and endings were often achieved with submission holds, like in amateur contests.

In 1999, there were more than 1,400 cards promoted by about 30 promotions in Japan, a nation approximately the size of the state of California. In addition to shoot wrestling leagues, there were organizations specifically devoted to lucha libre and women's wrestling, as well as groups like Frontier Martial Arts where bloody matches were the specialty. This type of "hardcore" wrestling—in which participants smash each other through tables, brawl in the crowd, and tie each other up in barbed wire— also moved to the United States. In 1998, the WWF introduced its own hardcore championship.

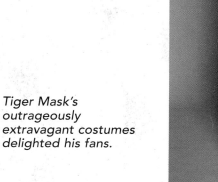

Tiger Mask's outrageously extravagant costumes delighted his fans.

As for Baba and Inoki, they stayed in business despite the changes, sometimes promoting cards with talent from the other leagues. Inoki was elected to the Japanese Diet—Japan's equivalent of the U. S. Senate—in 1989. And in 1995, he wrestled Ric Flair in front of 190,000 fans in North Korea, the birthplace of Rikidozan. Among the special guests at ringside was Inoki's old foe, Muhammad Ali. Baba continued to wrestle until 1998, when he was 60 years old and, many believe, already suffering from cancer. When he died in early 1999, the country seemed to stop. He was given a hero's funeral as more than 200 reporters waited outside. So many condolences were sent to both the All-Japan office and Baba's family that Japan's main telegraph company had to close.

It had run out of paper.

Lucha Libre

Mexican professional wrestling—known as "lucha libre," or "free fight"—has been enormously popular since 1933, when Salvador Lutteroth promoted the first card for his Consejo Mundial de Lucha Libre (World Lucha Libre Council) promotion, or CMLL. By the late 1990s, CMLL, sometimes also known by the initials EMLL, was running 10 shows a day and competing with organizations like AAA and Promo Azteca. Every major city had at least one wrestling school, with some students as young as 12 years old.

To the American eye, lucha libre may be difficult to follow. Mexican wrestlers tend to work from the right side of the body—applying a headlock while standing to an opponent's left—while Americans generally take the opposite posture. The most popular types of matches are six-man tag team bouts consisting of three wrestlers on each side: a captain and two members of the team. Wrestlers get in and out of the ring, often without tagging, with all six men frequently battling at once. There are many spectacular highlights before the finish of the match but the storytelling can be confusing. Victory is attained when either two members of a team or the captain is defeated. There are two referees, and two pinfalls regularly occur in the ring at the same time.

The battles are usually between "rudos," villains who brawl their way through their matches, and "technicos," who wrestle based on traditional maneuvers. A rudo will wrestle as a technico occasionally to prove that he's capable of more than dirty fighting. From time to time, a card will also feature special matches in which enemies join forces for one night only.

The mask is a symbol of honor among Mexican wrestlers. The country's biggest wrestling stars—El Canek, Mil Mascaras, and Blue Demon, among others—all wore masks. When two hooded grapplers feud, the loser often has to unmask. If neither man is masked, the wrestlers' hair may be at stake.

Like the Japanese, Mexican wrestlers are generally smaller than Americans, leading to matches marked by sensational high-flying moves. Many Mexican cards also include matches between highly athletic midgets.

Among the lucha libre moves incorporated into American pro wrestling are dives from the ring to the arena floor called "topes" (tow PAYS); the "huracanrana," a maneuver requiring the athlete to leap into the air, grab a foe with his feet, and twirl him to the mat; and "planchas," which involve a wrestler flying off the ropes to flatten an opponent.

9

The Murder of Bruiser Brody

Like Japan and Mexico, Puerto Rico has a long wrestling tradition. In the 1980s, the island was the home of the World Wrestling Council (WWC), as well as numerous opposition groups. WWC matches were known as bloody affairs, with fans taking the action very seriously. In fact, wrestlers who have appeared in Puerto Rico talk about the eerie feeling they get when spectators suddenly grow silent. "That means you leave the ring," said Abdullah the Butcher, one of the mat game's most infamous brawlers. "When the fans in Puerto Rico are quiet, it means they're going to riot."

In 1988, the WWC was running shows at arenas and stadiums around the island. But a dressing room murder would threaten the company's survival and taint the way the WWC was perceived by both fans and wrestlers.

The victim of the assault was one of the most independent wrestlers to ever perform. Bruiser Brody was a top attraction in both Japan and Puerto Rico, but American promoters hesitated sometimes to work with him. The 6-foot-5, 280-pound wildman did things on his own terms. If he did not approve of the way a promoter planned for a match to end, Brody changed the finish as he was wrestling, occasionally shocking his opponent by battering and pinning him.

The Bruiser

Brody's real name was Frank Goodish, and he was born in 1946 outside of Pittsburgh, Pennsylvania. In college, Goodish played football at Iowa State University and West Texas State University. After brief stints in the NFL and the Canadian Football League, Goodish ended up playing minor league football in San Antonio, Texas, and working as a sportswriter. It was during this period that he met Ivan Putski, a future member of the World Wrestling Federation Hall of Fame who was known as the Polish Strongman.

With Putski's help, Goodish became a wrestler, starting his career in Oklahoma. He then worked for Fritz Von Erich in Dallas, playing the role of a huge, crazy fan who came out of the stands to cause chaos. From Texas, the young wrestler traveled to Florida, where he met legendary villain Killer Kowalski in 1975. Kowalski told World Wide Wrestling Federation promoter Vince McMahon Sr. about Goodish's size and athleticism. McMahon renamed the grappler Bruiser Brody. With his long hair, beard, and growl, Brody was the type of heel many fans in WWWF cities such as New York, Boston, and Philadelphia enjoyed cheering.

But the wrestler did not like to follow orders. After a loud backstage argument with McMahon and wrestler Gorilla Monsoon, Brody left the WWWF for a promotion in New Zealand. In 1977, Von Erich brought his old attraction back to the United States. Fritz was in the final stages of his career and needed a rough-looking villain to sell his moves. Brody liked Von Erich and didn't mind losing to him.

The Murder of
Bruiser Brody

Bruiser Brody

    With Von Erich's help, Brody found work in other
territories associated with the NWA, particularly St.
Louis and Kansas City. In 1979, he made his first
tour of Japan and immediately became more popular than he'd ever been in the United States. Brody
entered the arena barking and swinging a chain.
When fans surged toward him, he chased them,
forcing them to scatter in all directions. The

Japanese wrestling magazines nicknamed him the Intelligent Monster because he was well spoken during interviews and appeared to understand wrestling strategy during his matches. Like Stan Hansen, another big American heel, Brody refused to do jobs in Japan, and promoter Shohei Baba agreed to the demand.

Brody made several more tours of Japan, then, in 1985, switched to Antonio Inoki's New Japan promotion. In one match, he squared off against 6-foot-5, 280-pound Seiji Sakaguchi, a former judo champion who was the company's "booker," the person who determines the finishes of matches and storylines. At some point, the match turned into a shoot, and Brody picked up his chair and rammed it into Sakaguchi's knee. The next day, Brody and partner Jimmy "Superfly" Snuka were on a train, heading to the finals of a tag team tournament in the city of Osaka. Still mad at Sakaguchi, Brody left the train with Snuka, leaving the promotion without a team for its big match. New Japan owed the wrestler $40,000, but he returned to America without bothering to collect the money. Once again, he proved to be a man who played by his own rules. Even money couldn't make Bruiser Brody do what he didn't want to.

Still, his services continued to be in demand. In 1987, he turned from heel to babyface in Puerto Rico when he saved Invader No. 1, a masked hero, from an attack by Abdullah the Butcher and partner Jason the Terrible. The fans who had screamed for Brody's destruction days earlier changed to loving the hairy American. But the promotion didn't always share the feeling.

Early in 1988, Brody was in a tag team match against the Japanese duo of Kendo Nagasaki and Mr. Pogo. Although Nagasaki and Pogo were champions in Puerto Rico, they rarely headlined cards in their own country. There were a number of Japanese photographers at ringside, and Brody decided that he didn't want his Japanese fans to see photos of Nagasaki and Pogo beating him up. When he got into the ring, he did not sell any of his opponents' moves and threw the two men around the ring whenever he felt like it.

WWC promoter—and top babyface—Carlos Colon was furious. He and the wrestler had a heated argument but eventually made up. Brody agreed to tour Puerto Rico again in the summer.

——————— *Death Match* ———————

On July 14, 1988, Brody began his visit by driving into San Juan with, among other people, Invader No. 1, whose real name was Jose Gonzales. Gonzales was the group's booker. If the promotion wanted Brody to do a job, Gonzales had to make the request. But there didn't seem to be any tension between the two on this day, as they made observations and jokes about the wrestling business.

Two days later, Brody was scheduled to wrestle another American, Danny Spivey, on a card at Juan Lobriel Stadium, in the city of Bayamón. There were

The masked Jose Gonzales wrestled under the name Invader No. 1.

Bruiser Brody subdues another foe.

two dressing rooms in the building—one for baby-faces and one for heels. Wrestlers who were in the babyface dressing room that night said Gonzales had a towel wrapped around his right hand when he asked Brody to step into the bathroom for a private conversation before his bout. Nobody heard what the two discussed. According to one theory, Gonzales asked Brody to do a job for Spivey and he refused. Others think the two may have clashed over money.

Shortly after the door closed, several wrestlers reportedly heard a scream. When they ran into the bathroom, they claimed that Brody was holding his bloody stomach. He had been stabbed through the lung, liver, and arteries.

Brody was taken to the hospital, where he died on the operating table at about 4 A. M. Gonzales, in the meantime, left the stadium with his shirt covered with blood. He returned later and wrestled his match. Two days later, he was arrested.

Death in the Ring

Wrestlers take particular offense when outsiders call their profession "fake" because stepping through the ropes can be a dangerous undertaking. Grapplers are constantly getting injured while trying to make their battles look realistic. On rare occasions, wrestlers have even died in the ring. Among the fatal cases:

July 2, 1969: Iron Mike DiBiase, the father of Million Dollar Man Ted DiBiase, died of a heart attack after wrestling Man Mountain Mike in Lubbock, Texas.

August 24, 1987: British legend Mal "King Kong" Kirk died after being splashed by 336-pound Shirley "Big Daddy" Crabtree in Great Yarmouth, England.

August 16, 1997: Japanese women's wrestler Plum Mariko died from head injuries sustained in a tag team match the day before.

May 23, 1999: Owen Hart died in an accident while being lowered from the ceiling at a WWF pay-per-view event.

Gonzales insisted that he'd acted in self-defense—a claim that didn't seem that outrageous, given Brody's unpredictable nature. What was curious was the way the Puerto Rican authorities handled the case. American wrestler Tony Atlas had been in the dressing room, but an order to bring him to Puerto Rico for the murder trial was never filed. Another wrestler, Dutch Mantell, was willing to testify, but his plane tickets didn't arrive until the trial ended. And the murder weapon was never found.

As a result, Gonzales was found not guilty. Brody's supporters claimed that the Puerto Rican system of justice was corrupt, allowing a killer with powerful connections to escape punishment.

Incredibly, Gonzales returned to action as Invader No. 1 in Puerto Rico. Once again, he was marketed as a babyface, even though the WWC was never as strong as it was before Brody's death.

10

SCANDAL

On April 1, 1990, World Wrestling Federation champion Hulk Hogan squared off against the Ultimate Warrior in the main event of "WrestleMania VI." More than 67,000 fans packed Toronto's SkyDome. Toward the end of the match, Hogan missed his usual finishing maneuver—a legdrop. As the "Hulkster" lay on the mat, the Warrior ran around the ring, bouncing off the ropes to pick up momentum. Then, the challenger splashed onto Hogan and pinned him, winning the WWF title.

The WWF had long-term plans for the Warrior, a long-haired, muscular wrestler named Jim Hellwig. He seemed to have the potential to replace Hogan as the group's top star. Before his matches, the Warrior would race down the aisle, exciting the fans as he jumped onto the ring apron and violently shook the ropes. The Warrior's best matches were short, when he exhibited power moves: lifting a man over his head and hurling him onto the mat, extending a rippling arm to deliver a "clothesline," slinging a foe off the ropes and zapping him with a foot to the face when he bounced back into the center of the ring. In a shoot, the Warrior would never stand a chance of getting down on the mat and exchanging amateur holds with former champions like Verne Gagne, Jack Brisco, or Bob Backlund. In the WWF of 1990, though, he seemed to have the ability to send the fans home excited.

Opposite page: The Ultimate Warrior couldn't beat Hogan outside of a wrestling ring.

Hulk Hogan raises the hand of the Ultimate Warrior after losing his title.

But the WWF quickly learned that the Ultimate Warrior was no Hulk Hogan. The new champion couldn't deliver an interview as well, and he didn't seem to bond with his audience the way Hogan did. People outside of wrestling generally did not regard the titlist as the same type of crossover celebrity.

In less than a year, the Warrior lost his belt to Sergeant Slaughter. Slaughter had been one of the WWF's biggest draws before the Hulk Hogan era, playing a patriotic Marine willing to sacrifice everything for his country. Then, he pretended to become a traitor. On January 16, 1991, U. S. troops launched air and missile attacks on Iraq after its leader, Saddam Hussein, ordered the invasion of neighboring Kuwait. Slaughter told fans that he no longer liked being an American and that he had won the title for Saddam. Hogan announced that he would win back the championship for the United States at "WrestleMania VII," to be held in Los Angeles on March 24, 1991.

The pairing seemed uneven. Slaughter was several years past his prime, and few expected him to win. By the time "WrestleMania VII" took place and Hogan won his third WWF championship, the war with Iraq had ended, lessening the interest. Some fans were offended that the WWF would use a war in which Americans had lost their lives to promote a pay-per-view event. The wrestling craze that started with the rock 'n' roll connection was clearly in trouble.

—— WWF's Problems Continue ——

Behind the scenes, the organization had other problems. In 1991, Dr. George Zahorian went on trial in Harrisburg, Pennsylvania, for selling anabolic steroids to, among others, WWF wrestlers. Anabolic steroids contain the male hormone testosterone. Athletes who have used the drug credit it with helping them increase strength and muscle mass and with reducing recovery time between workouts. "I had a 54-inch chest," said Superstar Billy Graham, the WWF champion from April 30, 1977, to February 20, 1978. "I used to be able to bench press over 600 pounds. Not too many people could do that. You can't accomplish anywhere near those statistics or those measurements without steroids. It's just impossible."

But steroids can also lead to serious health problems, including damage of the liver, kidneys, testicles, heart, and bones. After using steroids for about 20 years, Graham could barely walk. "What I have is called avascular necrosis, which means death of the bone joints," he said in 1993. "When you use steroids for a prolonged length of time, in large quantities, such as I did, it shuts off the blood supply to the joint, especially the hips and the ankles. It clogs up the blood vessels and the capillaries. Without the blood supply going to those joints, the bone literally dies."

Arnold Schwarzenegger admires the physique of Superstar Billy Graham.

Zahorian, a ringside physician at WWF events in Pennsylvania, was accused of breaking the law by supplying steroids to almost any wrestler interested in purchasing them. According to former WWWF champion Bruno Sammartino, the doctor set up shop in the dressing room. "[He] would come in with two bags, one with his medical supplies, and one with this stuff. The guys would get in a line to get the 'goodies.' "

At the trial, wrestlers like Rick Martel, B. Brian Blair, and Rowdy Roddy Piper admitted receiving steroids from Zahorian. Graham took the stand and told the jury about the horrors of steroid addiction: "When you go off steroids, you get a tremendous depression. You get tremendous thoughts of suicide. You go through a horrible withdrawal, and an extremely emotional psychological withdrawal. Because steroids make you feel so strong and so good and so confident, it makes you feel like you can conquer the world. And it is in your brain. And when it leaves your brain, you just feel so depressed."

Zahorian was convicted of selling anabolic steroids on June 27, 1991, and sentenced to three years in prison. Authorities continued to examine his relationship with the WWF, particularly after he testified that he sold the drugs to both Vince McMahon Jr.—who was a bodybuilder in his spare time—and Hulk Hogan.

The press picked up the story. To slow the frenzy, Hogan appeared on *The Arsenio Hall Show,* a late night television program, and claimed that he'd only used steroids on a few occasions. Wrestlers who had traveled with Hogan said he was lying. And Hogan himself would later testify that he started using steroids in 1976—before entering the WWF—and stopped in 1989. McMahon also admitted to experimenting with steroids but pledged to introduce testing for the drugs in the WWF.

Still, the controversy would not fade. A number of former wrestlers described the WWF as an organization filled with steroid addicts and McMahon as a boss who encouraged the use of the dangerous drugs. "Everybody used steroids," claimed former WWF Intercontinental champion Ken Patera. "If you didn't use them, you couldn't work for McMahon. He wanted everyone to look like a cartoon character."

Said Sammartino, "In the WWF, there used to be a joke. The joke was, if you didn't test positive for steroids, you were fired."

There were other scandals brewing. In 1992, two young men who had worked as "ring boys," carrying the wrestlers' robes and title belts from the ring to the dressing room, claimed that WWF employees had sexually molested them. Two of the accused individuals resigned from the organization.

Hulk Hogan testified that he took steroids.

Pro Wrestling

Ric Flair—in living color

Investigators conducted an 18-month probe into the allegations and concluded that there was not enough evidence to charge anyone with a crime.

When officials examined the steroid controversy, though, the outcome was different. On November 23, 1993, prosecutors charged that McMahon "conspired to distribute anabolic steroids to WWF wrestling performers to enhance their size and muscle development" between 1985 and 1991. He faced eight years in jail and a $500,000 fine. If McMahon was convicted, the government planned to seize the WWF's $9-million headquarters.

McMahon claimed the government was trying "to turn my personal life into a crime. [The prosecutors] claim that I shared some . . . steroids with a friend, and that somehow made me a dealer."

The legal concerns were taking their toll. McMahon couldn't concentrate on developing new wrestling plots and characters, and some of the WWF's decisions seemed careless. Ric Flair had joined the WWF. Throughout the 1980s, fans had wanted to see a "dream match" between the Nature

Boy and Hogan. But the WWF did not take the time to build up the clash. The two were placed in the ring quickly, and there was little of the expected fanfare. Flair won when Hogan was counted out.

Interest in the WWF was declining. In 1994, when McMahon's trial began, the WWF was seen on about 200 television stations—100 fewer than three years earlier.

The most dramatic moment of the proceedings occurred when Hogan was forced to testify. He said that the "vast majority" of WWF wrestlers had used steroids in the 1980s, and he and McMahon had shared the drug. Hogan also stated that he picked up steroids, along with his fan mail and paycheck, when he visited the WWF's headquarters. But he insisted that McMahon never ordered wrestlers to take steroids and didn't pay for the athletes' drugs.

On July 22, 1994, after 16 hours of deliberation, a jury found McMahon not guilty. The jurors concluded that even though McMahon had used steroids himself, there was no conspiracy.

Upon hearing the news, wrestling fans in the courtroom burst into cheers, while the promoter cried and hugged his wife and lawyers. "I'm elated," McMahon told the press. "Just like in wrestling, the good guys always win."

Vince McMahon and his wife leave the courtroom after he was acquitted.

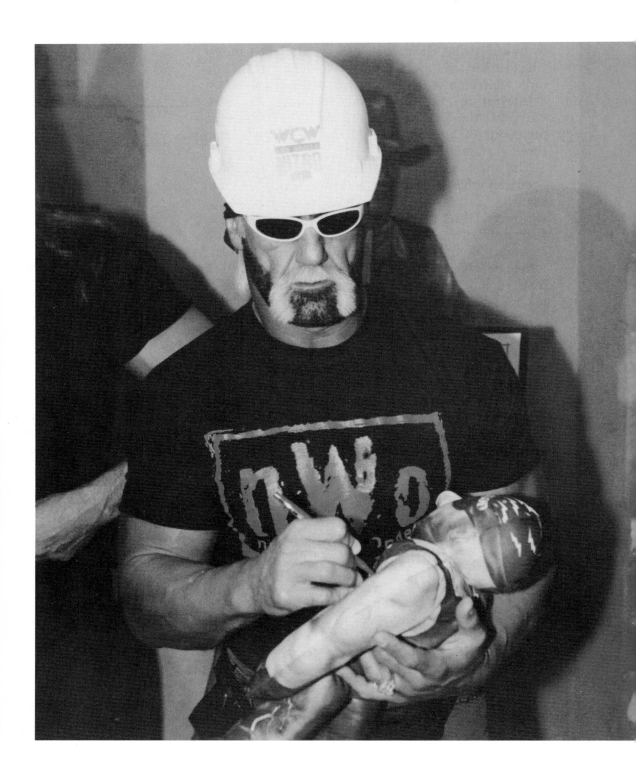

11

The New World Order

Around the same time that the WWF was experiencing legal troubles, it encountered another problem. For the first time in several years, it faced real competition from a rival wrestling organization. It began when Jim Crockett, the only major American promoter left in the NWA, realized that he could no longer battle Vince McMahon by himself. In 1988, he sold his promotion to Ted Turner, owner of professional baseball's Atlanta Braves and pro basketball's Atlanta Hawks.

Turner—who had started the Goodwill Games, an international sports competition similar to the Olympics, and donated millions of dollars to charity—also owned numerous cable television networks, including TBS, TNT, CNN, and the Cartoon Network. Wrestling had always been one of the most popular programs on TBS, the network Turner had started in Georgia and turned into a "superstation" seen all over the United States. Because pro wrestling had helped TBS draw new viewers, Turner reportedly felt a sense of loyalty to the wrestlers and didn't want to see the promotion die.

Turner may have had another motive also. In 1984, the WWF had briefly appeared on TBS.

Opposite page: Hulk Hogan added Hollywood to his name when he joined the New World Order.

Turner and McMahon had different ideas about how to present the program, and the two men clashed. Within nine months, the WWF was no longer seen on any of Turner's stations, and bitterness remained on both sides. With Turner's acquisition of NWA, Turner and McMahon would be direct competitors.

—— WCW Gets into the Act ——

Turner's promotion went by the name World Championship Wrestling (WCW). For the first few years after the purchase, the NWA champion continued to defend his title on WCW shows. But in 1993, WCW removed itself from the small group of promotions still associated with the NWA. Although the NWA championship continued to exist, it was mainly defended on cards staged in little gymnasiums. On Turner's programs, the most important title became the WCW heavyweight belt. The majority of old NWA fans accepted this change and considered the WCW championship part of the tradition linked to the old NWA.

With his numerous other business interests, Turner did not have the time to be involved in the day-to-day decisions of WCW. Instead, a number of executives oversaw the wrestling division of Turner's empire. The one who had the greatest impact on WCW, and the wrestling industry as a whole, was Eric Bischoff.

Like Turner, Bischoff also had reasons to dislike McMahon. Bischoff had been an agricultural equipment manager when he met Verne Gagne, the head of the old American Wrestling Association (AWA). Gagne liked Bischoff and hired him as a television announcer. But by the end of 1990, the AWA was on the decline, and Bischoff had larger goals. At one point, he auditioned for an announcer's position with the WWF. McMahon was unimpressed with the dark-haired, boyish commentator. Bischoff did not get the job, but he would eventually gain a measure of revenge against the man who had rejected him.

Starting in WCW as an announcer, Bischoff made friends with people in the Turner organization. Soon, he was managing the company's wrestling operations. While other WCW executives had tried to catch up to the WWF, Bischoff's aim was to overtake the leading league.

In June 1994, Bischoff helped lure the man many considered the symbol of the WWF, Hulk Hogan, to WCW. Bischoff accomplished this goal by promising Hogan a huge salary, along with a sizable percentage of pay-per-view fees. Hogan had already appeared in several films and television shows, and the Turner organization also promised to help him pursue his acting career. Plus, he wouldn't have to travel as much as the other wrestlers, allowing him to spend more time with his family.

Behind the scenes, Ric Flair also helped arrange the deal. He and Hogan had been competitors for years. Flair represented the NWA when Hogan was the star of the WWF. The men had been opponents in the WWF, and each had opinions about the way the wrestling business should be run. Flair believed that a feud pitting Hogan against Flair, or against other WCW stars, would rivet fans. Some of these fans might even abandon the WWF because they found WCW more interesting.

With Hogan gone, Randy "Macho Man" Savage was left as the best-known WWF wrestler. When Savage was interviewed about the situation, he claimed to be surprised by Hogan's choice, comparing the WWF to baseball's major leagues and WCW to the minors. Savage praised McMahon as a boss and a person, creating sympathy for the WWF owner as he battled through the steroid trial. But by December, WCW had made Savage such a generous offer that he also joined the group.

Savage's ex-wife, Elizabeth, who was his manager during his greatest WWF matches, had left the wrestling business. But the WCW lured her, too. She would play the role of a greedy woman who happily spent the money she'd received in her divorce settlement with the superstar. Rowdy Roddy Piper— Hogan's archenemy during the time of the first

Ric Flair goes flying.

"WrestleMania"—and managers Jimmy "the Mouth of the South" Hart, Bobby "The Brain" Heenan, and Million Dollar Man Ted DiBiase shifted alliances as well. The aim was to convince fans that anyone who had meant anything during the WWF's strongest period no longer wanted to be there. WCW, according to its ads, was "where the big boys play."

WCW vs. the WWF

In 1995, Bischoff fired another shot at McMahon, starting a Monday night wrestling program called *Monday Nitro* on Turner's TNT cable network. The show would run opposite the WWF's *Monday Night Raw* (later *Raw is War*) on the USA cable station. Even people in WCW wondered if Bischoff was being too aggressive. Was having two major wrestling programs on at the same time good for the business? Some feared that fans would get frustrated switching channels, then lose interest in wrestling entirely. But Bischoff had already hurt McMahon, and he advised Turner to hit the WWF owner with more ammunition.

The first *Monday Nitro,* televised from the Mall of America in Minnesota on September 4, 1995, featured a major surprise. WWF star Lex Luger appeared, dressed in street clothes. Luger made several negative comments about the WWF, then demanded a title shot against Hogan, who had beaten Flair for the WCW heavyweight title in July 1994. The routine shocked the WWF's stable of wrestlers. They'd seen Luger the previous weekend when he wrestled for the WWF in Canada. Apparently, nobody realized that he was planning to switch sides and embarrass the organization.

The "Monday Night Wars" had begun. The WWF did a series of skits making fun of Turner, Hogan, and Savage. "Billionaire Ted" was a dopey business-man who doled out huge sums of cash to "the Huckster" and "Nacho Man"—wrestlers too old to be in the ring. WCW responded with its own tricks, announcing the results of matches the WWF taped before those bouts were shown on *Raw*. World Wrestling Federation women's champion Alundra Blayze walked onto the set of *Nitro* and tossed her belt into a garbage can, branding the WWF title as worthless.

On May 27, 1996, Scott Hall—then known to fans as WWF star Razor Ramon—emerged from the *Nitro* audience to declare war on WCW. On June 10, he was joined on the program by Kevin Nash, who, under the name Diesel, had held the WWF championship from November 26, 1994, to November 19, 1995. Nash and Hall pretended that they were not under contract to WCW. Instead, they acted like two thugs who had come over from the WWF just to harass people. The announcers called the pair the Outsiders and seemed genuinely frightened of them whenever they intruded on the program. On June 16, the Outsiders added to the fear by attacking one of the announcers—Bischoff—and slamming him through the interview stage.

Several weeks later, at WCW's "Bash at the Beach" pay-per-view event, Nash and Hall revealed a third member of the Outsiders: Hogan. As spectators bombarded the ring with garbage, Hogan—calling himself Hollywood Hulk Hogan—mocked the fans who had cheered him through the years. "I did it for the money," he said.

The trio renamed their group the N. W. O. for "New World Order." The N. W. O. acted like a renegade organization that was operating in WCW. They pretended not to respect the organization's titles or feel bound by its rules. Although they were supposed to be heels, members were wildly cheered by fans who approved of the N. W. O.'s outlaw style.

Each week, others joined the N. W. O: Savage, former WCW champion Sting, Lex Luger, the Giant (7-foot Paul Wight, who started his career billed as Andre the Giant's son) and Bischoff himself. Dennis Rodman, the most colorful player in the National Basketball Association, also became part of the group, teaming with Hogan and once missing basketball practice to take part in a wrestling show. Popular late-night talk show host Jay Leno starred

"*I did it for the money.*"

Dennis Rodman, left, Hulk Hogan, center, and Karl Malone, right, surround an overmatched Jay Leno during an appearance on The Late Show.

on a WCW pay-per-view in 1998, teaming with wrestler Diamond Dallas Page against the N. W. O. duo of Hogan and Bischoff.

Eventually the faction became so crowded that it splintered off into the Wolfpac, headed by Nash, and the N. W. O. Black and White, led by Hogan. A collection of Hispanic wrestlers formed L. W. O., the Latino World Order. Fueled largely by the success of the N. W. O., *Nitro* managed to outdraw *Raw* for more than a year and a half.

Meanwhile, WCW was also developing new stars, among them Bill Goldberg, who had played football for the University of Georgia and the Atlanta Falcons. After injuries forced him to quit football, Goldberg ran into Diamond Dallas Page at an Atlanta nightclub. Page convinced the athlete to sign up for the Power Plant, the WCW training school.

With his shaved head, goatee, and muscular physique, Goldberg—billed as 6-foot-3 and 285 pounds—made his television debut on September 22, 1997, against Hugh Morrus. Morrus seemed to have his opponent beaten after delivering the "No Laughing Matter" moonsault, a maneuver in which a wrestler climbs to the top turnbuckle and back-flips onto his opponent. To the fans' amazement, Goldberg recovered from the move, then defeated Morrus by gripping him around the waist, turning him upside down, and driving his back into the can-vas. The move—sometimes called the "jackham-mer"—was renamed the "Goldberg Spear."

For much of the next year, Goldberg plowed his way through the other wrestlers, winning many of his matches in less than a minute. On July 7, 1998, at Atlanta's Georgia Dome, Hogan lost the WCW heavyweight title to the 32-year-old rookie sensation.

Like Hogan, Goldberg was the type of wrestler who appealed to both fans and non-fans. He had the right look for television, he created a mood of inten-sity, and he was very well spoken. After the win, articles about Goldberg appeared in such magazines as *The New Yorker* and *People.*

But while the WCW champion was receiving his praise, the WWF was making a comeback. Vince McMahon had come up with a new way of grabbing the public's attention. And, as in the past, it involved redefining the wrestling business.

12

ATTITUDE

In 1992, a new promotion started in Philadelphia, operating out of a bingo hall and offering fans a type of wrestling they couldn't find in the WWF or WCW. The group—eventually known as Extreme Championship Wrestling (ECW)—featured crazy, bloody brawls, mixed with lightning-quick acrobatic displays and spicy plots. Fans carried weapons like frying pans and barbecue tongs into the arena, handing the objects to the wrestlers as they fought at ringside. Female valets and managers wore revealing outfits and often exchanged blows with male wrestlers. Barbed wire and fire surrounded the ring during some matches. And the performers seemed willing to do anything to thrill the crowd.

Men like Cactus Jack, Sabu, and Taz launched themselves off of tables, ladders, and folding chairs onto their opponents and took dives off the top rope onto the arena floor. After several years in WCW, future WWF champion Steve Austin entered ECW, amusing fans by doing insulting imitations of Eric Bischoff. The Sandman strolled to the ring while drinking beer and smoking cigarettes, then bashed his foes with a bamboo cane. Other performers, like Eddy Guerrero, Dean Malenko, and Chris Benoit, put on the type of highly athletic aerial displays more common in Mexican and Japanese rings than in the United States.

Opposite page: Mick Foley wrestled under the names "Cactus Jack" and "Mankind."

An ECW pay-per-view, shown on March 21, 1999, provided an example of ECW's brand of excitement. In a fast-moving match, Mexico's Super Crazy lay on his back and used his feet to propel his Japanese opponent, Yoshihiro Tajiri, over the ropes. Then Crazy stepped onto the ring apron, hopped to the second strand, and backflipped onto his foe. Later in the card, New Jack taped his former tag team partner, Mustafa, to a table before climbing into the balcony and diving onto his chest. In the main event, Sabu leaped to the top rope from a chair set up in the middle of the ring, propelling himself at Taz, who—standing on the arena floor—picked up another chair, which he used to crack his opponent in the head.

From Philadelphia, ECW expanded to New York, Florida, and other places. Although they didn't put on shows in as many cities as the WWF and WCW and filled smaller arenas, the group developed a loyal following. Fans who could not receive ECW broadcasts in their hometowns purchased and traded videotapes of the rebel promotion.

At first, both the WWF and WCW claimed that ECW's rough style was too distasteful for most fans. But both groups seemed to be influenced by this promotion. WWF and WCW wrestlers began using more daring maneuvers, and ECW talent began to be lured away to the rival organizations. The Sandman—later called Hak—Malenko, and Benoit went to WCW. Cactus Jack (also known as Mankind) and Austin ended up in the WWF.

The WWF'S New Tactics

ECW's growing following indicated that society and wrestling fans were changing. Spectators wanted more than the traditional good guy vs. bad guy feud. WCW had proven this when the N. W. O. members were cheered more loudly than the babyfaces. The WWF watched these trends and decided to outdo both WCW and ECW. In April 1997, after its Monday night ratings had hit their lowest point, the WWF began introducing fans to new plots.

For years, Bret "Hit Man" Hart had been one of the WWF's top babyfaces. But he began telling American fans what he thought of their country. The native of Calgary, in Canada's province of Alberta, described the United States as a country that "glorifies criminal conduct." On one WWF broadcast, he stood in the center of the ring and proclaimed, "Canada's a country where we still take care of the sick and the old, where we still have health care. We got gun control. We don't kill each other and shoot each other on every street corner. Canada isn't riddled with racial prejudice and hatred."

Hart didn't have to work hard to deliver these comments. He was genuinely sickened by many of the negative influences he saw in the United States. Many American fans were offended that a Canadian would have the nerve to deliver sermons about the ills of their country. But Canadians were overjoyed to hear one of their countrymen telling Americans what they deserved to hear. As a result of this controversy, Hart became a heel in the United States and the number one babyface in Canada.

The Hit Man was also the World Wrestling Federation heavyweight champion and hoped to remain with the organization as a front office advisor after he retired. However, Vince McMahon had second thoughts about a deal they'd made and decided that he could not afford to pay Hart's high salary. Bret received permission to negotiate with WCW, and the rival league quickly signed him.

U.S. fans loved to hate Canadian Bret Hart.

McMahon was concerned that Hart would appear in WCW with the WWF championship. He remembered how WWF women's titlist Alundra Blayze had gone on a WCW program and tossed her belt into a garbage can. It was an embarrassing moment for the WWF, and McMahon had no intention of allowing Hart to do the same thing.

The Hit Man insisted he would never do something that humiliating to McMahon, a man he had described as a second father. But when McMahon asked the champion to drop the title to Shawn Michaels at an upcoming pay-per-view in Montreal,

Hart declined. Besides personally disliking Michaels, Hart did not want to lose his championship in front of a Canadian crowd. He offered to hand the belt to McMahon the next day on the WWF's Monday night program, *Raw is War.* McMahon agreed to let the Montreal match end in a disqualification, but he was still worried that Hart would appear on WCW's *Nitro* show with the title instead of on *Raw.*

On November 9, 1997, Hart and Michaels had their match in Montreal. As the bout appeared to be warming up, Michaels caught Hart in the "sharpshooter," the leglock that Hart had made famous. It involves a wrestler laying an opponent on his chest, tying both of his opponent's legs over his thighs, and applying pressure. The Hit Man believed that he was soon going to break out of the hold and apply his own sharpshooter on Michaels. Then, the plan was that the match would continue until Hart's brother, Owen Hart, and other allies rushed into the ring, causing a disqualification. Since a title cannot change hands on a disqualification, Bret Hart would leave Montreal as the champion.

But Hart never had a chance to burst free of the sharpshooter. Unexpectedly, the referee signaled for the bell to ring—as if Hart had submitted to the hold. McMahon was sitting at ringside and also demanded that the timekeeper ring the bell. Michaels was declared the champion. Hart stormed back to the dressing room where McMahon met him. He knew Bret was mad, but the WWF was McMahon's company, and he believed that he had done what was necessary to protect its championship.

When the dressing room doors closed, Hart slugged McMahon but the altercation was quickly broken up. McMahon had no regrets about showing the other wrestlers that he was willing to take a punch for what he thought was proper. "I just screwed Bret," McMahon said. "And I did it for the World Wrestling Federation. I did it for me. I did it for all the performers who stayed behind after Bret left. And I would do it again tomorrow because it was the right thing to do."

Bret Hart early in his career

Word about the double-cross spread quickly through the Internet, wrestling newsletters, and other sources. When McMahon entered arenas, fans loyal to Hart booed him. Rather than ignore the jeers, the WWF owner decided to profit from them. He portrayed himself as a heel promoter who could crush a wrestler's dreams with one decision. Of all the wrestlers in the WWF, only one was depicted as bold enough to take on his boss. That was the new star of the organization: Stone Cold Steve Austin.

———— A Stone Cold Star ————

Austin was born Steve Williams on December 18, 1965, and grew up in the small town of Edna, Texas. After graduating from high school, he attended Wharton County Junior College, outside Houston, then North Texas State University on a football scholarship. When his scholarship ran out, he got a job loading and unloading trucks. One day, while watching the local World Class Wrestling Association on television, he saw a commercial for its wrestling school. Williams enrolled and five months later, in 1990, debuted in World Class.

A wrestler named Steve Williams was already headlining arenas in the southern United States and Japan, so the rookie became Steve Austin. In 1991, he joined WCW. With his long blond hair and riveting interview style, some predicted that he would become the next Ric Flair. He and Brian Pillman formed a memorable tag team called the Hollywood Blonds. But he and the WCW couldn't agree on a gimmick that would turn him into a singles star. While recuperating from a tricep injury, Austin said the company fired him.

ECW soon hired Austin. Because he was still recovering, he only wrestled a few matches. His explosive interview style caught the attention of the WWF, and he signed with the organization in 1995.

Interestingly, the man who would become one of the WWF's most unforgettable speakers was assigned another performer to do the talking for

Bret Hart

him. Austin was given the nickname the Ringmaster and was managed by Million Dollar Man Ted DiBiase. DiBiase always delivered an exceptional interview. Despite his respect for DiBiase's skills, Austin believed that the situation would not advance his career. "Nobody knows what you can do until they put a microphone in front of you and a camera on you and give you a chance," Austin said. By 1996, Austin and DiBiase had parted ways, and the wrestler was coming into his own. He won the WWF's "King of the Ring" tournament, defeating Jake "the Snake" Roberts in the finals. Like DiBiase, Roberts had been a WWF star in the 1980s. Then he'd experienced a number of personal problems—particularly alcoholism—and became very religious. He frequently told listeners to open their Bibles to John 3:16, the section of the New Testament stating that those who believe in Jesus Christ will have everlasting life. Upon winning the "King of the Ring," Austin took the microphone and told fans that they should study "Austin 3:16."

Stone Cold Steve Austin promotes his "gospel."

. . .former heavyweight boxing champion Mike Tyson was the "special enforcer" in the match, in charge of keeping order.

Austin was supposed to be a heel. He used foul language and seemed not to care whether spectators cheered or booed him. But the fans liked his independent attitude and the fact that, unlike wrestling heroes of the past, he made no effort to be liked. A feud with Bret Hart only increased his popularity. Since American fans hated the Hit Man, they applauded his opponent.

On August 3, 1997, Austin suffered a serious neck injury in a match against Bret's brother, Owen. Fans learned that this was not an act and cheered Austin's bravery when he made a comeback. Then, on March 29, 1998, Austin—called Stone Cold Steve Austin—won his first WWF heavyweight championship from Shawn Michaels at "WrestleMania XIV." The bout received international attention because former heavyweight boxing champion Mike Tyson was the "special enforcer" in the match, in charge of keeping order. In the closing moments, Tyson assisted Austin, making him an even bigger star.

Austin was a pure babyface. And McMahon used the champion's popularity to make himself into a bigger heel. First, the promoter infuriated spectators by insisting that Austin wear a suit and tie and become a "corporate" champion. When Austin refused, McMahon said that he was dedicating himself to ruining the disobedient wrestler's career. Austin's response was beating up his boss—a fantasy many fans wanted to act out on their own employers.

On one broadcast, the wrestler attacked McMahon while the promoter lay in a hospital bed. Another time, the pair met in a cage. As they climbed the outside of the pen, Austin bashed the owner's head against the bars. McMahon fell backward, crashing through an announcer's table.

Austin represented what the organization called the new, tougher WWF attitude, and the formula worked. WWF ratings soared, and *Raw* became the most popular program on cable television—setting a record on May 10, 1999, with 6,156,000 viewers. A compact disc of entrance music played at WWF arenas became a best-seller. Wrestlers were regular guest stars on other TV shows. The WWF opened a theme restaurant and store in New York City's Times Square. An autobiography by wrestler Mick "Mankind" Foley was on *The New York Times* best-sellers list.

However, critics of professional wrestling believed the WWF was sending young people very negative messages: settle your differences with violence, and don't listen to authority. In 1999, Indiana University released a study of 50 separate episodes of *Raw.* The researchers found that, on a typical two-hour program, there were only 36 minutes of wrestling. The rest of the show was devoted to interviews and skits, building interest in storylines that some felt were not appropriate for children. During the period surveyed, the study noted 609 incidents involving the use of garbage cans, tables, chairs, and brooms as weapons, 273 kicks to the groin, and 157 instances of fans and wrestlers displaying their middle finger.

McMahon responded to the criticism by saying that his programs were not any more shocking than many other things watched by young people. "We settle our differences physically in a wrestling ring," he argued. "How bad is that compared to a [Arnold] Schwarzenegger or [Sylvester] Stallone movie?" Besides, he said, it was the responsibility of parents to determine their children's viewing habits, not Vince McMahon or the WWF.

But he also admitted that the WWF liked being thought of as the bad boys of television because it meant that the company stood apart from its competitors. "Some of the controversy that's created," he conceded, "is controversy we actually create." No one was prepared, however, when the WWF suffered its most distressing controversy.

Jesse "The Body" Ventura

In the middle of professional wrestling's greatest wave of popularity, former grappler and announcer Jesse "The Body" Ventura was elected governor of Minnesota. As Ventura put it, "We shocked the world."

Ventura was born James George Janos in Minneapolis, Minnesota, in 1951. He excelled in high school sports and became a member of the elite Navy SEALs—an abbreviation for Sea, Air, and Land forces—specializing in underwater demolition, among other difficult tasks. The young man served in the Vietnam War, as well as on missions throughout Asia. After leaving the Navy in 1973, he trained to become a professional wrestler. He modeled his style after Superstar Billy Graham, the smooth-talking bleached blond muscleman who held the World Wide Wrestling Federation championship from April 1977 to February 1978.

Janos decided to take the name Jesse because he had always liked it. He looked at a map of California, saw the city of Ventura, and decided he had found a last name. At 6-foot-4 and 260 pounds, Ventura was a colorful presence, flexing his arms and uttering memorable phrases during interviews. With Adrian Adonis, he won the American Wrestling Association (AWA) tag team championship in 1980, then journeyed to the WWF.

In 1985, Ventura was scheduled to challenge Hulk Hogan, then the WWF champion, in Los Angeles. A few days before the match, Ventura developed blood clots on his lung. Doctors dissolved the clots, but Ventura wanted to do something while he recovered. Realizing that he was a great speaker, the WWF made him an announcer on its broadcasts. Often, he appeared alongside Vince McMahon on the group's programs, poking fun at the promoter.

Fans cheered Ventura when he criticized the WWF's top babyfaces, claiming that he was simply "telling it like it is." His wrestling fame allowed him to provide commentary for Minnesota Vikings and Tampa Bay Buccaneers football games and appear in action films such as *Predator* and *The Running Man.*

Chyna decorates Minnesota's wrestling governor, Jesse Ventura.

After leaving the WWF in 1990, Ventura also announced for WCW.

In 1990, angry about a storm sewer project planned for a wetland near his home, Ventura ran for mayor of Brooklyn Park, Minnesota. He defeated the man who had held that office for 18 years, Jim Krautmeyer. After his term expired, the retired wrestler hosted a Minnesota radio program, mocking the government as being out of touch with the common person.

Ventura's opinions became so popular that the Reform Party—an alternative to the Democratic and Republican parties—recruited him to run for governor in 1998. None of the polls gave Ventura a chance against his opponents, Republican Norm Coleman—the mayor of the state's capital city, St. Paul—and Democrat "Skip" Humphrey, son of former Vice President Hubert Humphrey. Few political observers realized that Ventura's wrestling background had taught him how to rile up a crowd. He encouraged college students and other first-time voters to cast their ballots. Many of Ventura's supporters said that they rallied behind him because they remembered watching him as a wrestler and announcer.

Ventura claimed that the election result proved that democracy really works in the United States because anyone, even a former wrestler, could be elected. In the weeks after the election, he insisted that he was too busy to watch wrestling any more. But, less than a year after he was inaugurated, he returned to the ring as a special referee for the WWF "SummerSlam" pay-per-view event. Although his political opponents criticized the move as undignified, Ventura insisted that there was nothing wrong with a governor who "wanted to have fun."

13

A Sad Farewell

The name of the pay-per-view event shown on May 23, 1999, was "Over the Edge." On a card featuring matches like the Undertaker vs. Stone Cold Steve Austin and the Rock vs. Hunter Hearst Helmsley, the WWF also promised a bout between a wrestler called the Godfather and Bret Hart's brother, Owen.

According to the plot, Owen represented everyone disgusted with the new direction of the WWF. He told his audience that he believed in wrestling the way it was presented in the old days—a game featuring traditional "good guys" and "bad guys" exchanging holds. Owen's character was a spoof of the old-time wrestling good guy. He called himself the Blue Blazer, a masked superhero who wore a feathered costume and urged kids to take their vitamins and drink their milk.

Before his match at "Over the Edge," the Blazer was to be lowered to the ring from the ceiling of the Kemper Arena in Kansas City. But for some reason, Hart slipped out of his harness and fell a reported 90 feet, hitting his head on a turnbuckle and crashing onto the mat. At first, the fans thought this was part of the show. But almost immediately they realized that something was really wrong. They stood and

Opposite page: A young fan mourns the death of Owen Hart in the ring.

became quiet. Announcer Jim Ross was holding back tears when he told viewers, "This is not part of the entertainment portion of the show. This is as real as real can get."

Hart had severe internal injuries. Emergency medical technicians tried massaging his heart. When he was carried out of the building, the fans stood and gave the wrestler a standing ovation, hoping that he'd recover. But later in the show, Ross told viewers the terrible news: 34-year-old Owen Hart was dead.

——— *A Beloved Wrestler* ———

Owen Hart

Owen Hart was born on May 7, 1965, into one of the most colorful families in professional wrestling. His father was Stu Hart, the legendary wrestler and promoter from Calgary. Over the years, Stu Hart trained dozens of wrestlers in a cramped, paneled room called the Dungeon in his home. He was a tough shooter and, even when he was in his 80s, could tie up a student in an excruciating submission hold.

Like other wrestling fathers—including Bob Armstrong, Gory Guerrero, Jacques Rougeau Sr., and Fritz Von Erich—the elder Hart encouraged his sons to go into the family profession. Besides Owen and Bret, the other boys in the family—Bruce, Keith, Smith, Ross, and Wayne (an eighth brother, Dean, died of Bright's Disease, a kidney ailment)—also wrestled, mainly for Stu's Calgary-based Stampede promotion. All four of the Hart sisters—Diana, Ellie, Alison, and Georgia—married wrestlers. Among Stu's better-known sons-in-law: Jim "the Anvil" Neidhart and the British Bulldog Davey Boy Smith.

Dinner at the Hart home was usually a noisy occasion, with Stu telling stories about former New York promoter Toots Mondt or 1950s NWA champion Whipper Billy Watson. Occasionally, the old wrestler would rise from the table to demonstrate a hammerlock or armbar on a grandchild.

"Wrestling is the divine right of kings in this family," joked Bruce Hart. "Others are born with silver

Boxing great Rocky Marciano, center, meets the entire Hart family.

spoons in their mouths. We were born with silver turnbuckles in ours."

Owen, the youngest member of the Hart family, originally wanted to be a gym teacher. But he was such a gifted athlete that he began wrestling as a teenager. He worked hard at his craft, watching tapes of matches from different parts of the world and borrowing from the various styles. He also wrestled in England, Germany, and Japan, where he won the junior heavyweight title for Antonio Inoki's New Japan promotion in 1988, before joining the WWF.

Owen started out in the WWF as the Blue Blazer, the same masked character he was portraying when he died. His style was high-flying and athletic, featuring the dazzling types of maneuvers favored by lightweight wrestlers in Japan and Mexico. The gimmick didn't fascinate the public, and Owen left the WWF soon after, briefly wrestling in WCW, among other places. In 1991, he returned to the WWF using his real name.

The Curse of the Von Erichs

Few wrestling territories enjoyed the success of the Dallas-based World Class Wrestling Association. Promoter Fritz Von Erich's secrets included playing rock 'n' roll music when popular wrestlers entered the ring, a television show seen as far away as Israel, and a collection of young, handsome babyfaces composed largely of his sons. But as healthy as business was in World Class, the story of the Von Erichs is the most tragic in wrestling. Before they were 35 years old, five of Fritz's six sons were dead.

Fritz Von Erich started life as Jack Adkisson but transformed himself into the wrestling heel Fritz Von Erich in the 1950s. He played a Nazi soldier still loyal to Adolf Hitler, the German dictator who died in the final days of World War II. The routine made Von Erich into a star, and he won the AWA world championship in 1963.

But while Fritz was away touring, his family suffered their first crisis. When his oldest son, Jackie, was seven, he was playing near some exposed wires in the family's Niagara Falls, New York, trailer park. The boy was jolted by a surge of electricity, and fell, unconscious, into a pile of melting snow, where he drowned.

From left: Kevin, David, Fritz, and Kerry Von Erich

Mike Von Erich demonstrates the "Claw."

The death could not stop Von Erich's rise. He turned himself into a babyface and became a successful promoter and businessman. By the early 1980s, four of Von Erich's sons were his top attractions. They were marketed as all-American boys who valued God and their family. Six-foot-6 David Von Erich may have been the most athletic of the bunch. He entered the ring carrying a yellow rose, the symbol of Texas, and wearing a cowboy hat. His slim but muscular younger brother Kevin wrestled barefoot and was known for his aerial moves and dropkicks. An even younger brother, Kerry, was the brawniest of the boys. With his feathered hair and fringed ring jackets, he looked like a rock star and was billed as the Modern Day Warrior. A fourth brother, Mike, was not as athletic as his siblings, but he was still presented to the public as a superstar.

Although the World Class promotion was faring well with the Von Erich brothers as its stars, terrible drug problems plagued the promotion. And, one by one, the Von Erich brothers started to die. David was found dead in his hotel room in Japan in 1984. American newspapers reported that he'd died of injuries suffered from a kick during a match, but rumors spread that the real cause was drugs. By 1987, Mike had become addicted to tranquilizers and painkillers. A police officer pulled Mike over and found a variety of drugs inside his car. Mike committed suicide by taking an overdose of a sleeping medication called Placidyl several days later. The youngest Von Erich brother, Chris, entered the business, but he was frustrated that his size—he stood 5-feet-5 and weighed 165 pounds—and his asthma problems prevented him from achieving the same fame as the other Von Erichs. In 1991, he shot himself in the head. Then, in 1993, after a series of drug arrests, Kerry shot himself in the heart.

Of all the Von Erich boys, only Kevin survived. Some in wrestling directed their anger toward Fritz, claiming that he'd forced his sons into the wrestling business and ignored their drug problems. Before his death in 1997, Fritz responded to the accusations. "Some people say I pushed those boys into wrestling, and wrestling killed them—like I killed them," he said. "Killed them? I loved those boys. I didn't force them to be wrestlers....They wanted to be wrestlers. I helped them. But wrestling didn't kill them. Different things killed them."

He teamed with his brother-in-law, Jim "the Anvil" Neidhart, and another high flyer, Koko B. Ware. WWF fans were largely uninterested in Owen until he got involved in a "family feud" with brother Bret. Owen played the role of a jealous younger brother who blamed the shortcomings in his career on his older sibling.

The two finally met in the opening match of "WrestleMania X" in 1994. It was a thrilling exhibition, full of ambitious, acrobatic maneuvers. At the end of the bout, Bret hopped onto Owen's shoulders, preparing to hook his legs around his brother and wheel him forward onto the mat with a move called a "victory roll." But the Hit Man appeared to lose his balance, and Owen landed on top, pinning his older brother. Later that night, Bret emerged from the tournament as the WWF heavyweight champion, and Owen had become a top contender.

A few months later, the two had a rematch in a cage at the "SummerSlam" pay-per-view. As the Hart family watched from ringside, Bret and Owen fought on the outside of the enclosure. When Bret smashed his brother's head against the steel, Owen appeared to catch his ankles between the bars—allowing the Hit Man to scramble to the arena floor, winning the match.

In the audience, members of the Hart family began to brawl. Jim "the Anvil" Neidhart extended his arm and blasted fellow brother-in-law Davey Boy Smith from the rear with a clothesline, sending him and his wife, Diana, tumbling over the guardrail. Then, Neidhart and Owen dragged Bret back into the cage, padlocking the door and pounding on him until the other Hart brothers fought their way into the ring to rescue the Hit Man.

On November 11, 1994, the Hart clan was again at ringside when Bret defended his belt against former titlist Bob Backlund. At one point, Backlund apparently trapped the champion in a "chicken wing" hold, twisting back his arm and neck. Owen seemed to be concerned for his brother and urged his mother, Helen Hart, to surrender the match by tossing a towel into the ring. As soon as she followed Owen's request and the championship was awarded to Backlund, the younger Hart jumped for joy, maintaining his status as a hated heel.

In 1997, after Owen had held the tag team championship with both Yokozuna and the British Bulldog, the Hart brothers reunited, battling against Stone Cold Steve Austin and his allies in a U. S. A. vs. Canada feud. Owen won the World Wrestling Federation Intercontinental championship twice before Bret left the organization after his bitter conflict with McMahon. Owen remained with the WWF—winning the tag team title with Jeff Jarrett as well as the European belt. However, Owen was reportedly thinking about retirement.

"When my contract is up, I'm out of wrestling," he said shortly before his death. "I've been smart . . . Financially, I'm set . . . I need to start focusing on my family and letting go of wrestling."

The Controversy

"When I think about Owen's life," sobbed Jeff Jarrett, Owen's tag team partner at the time of his death, as he arrived in Calgary for Owen's funeral, "I think about integrity. Because in this business, it's cold . . . it's selfish . . . it's unrealistic, it's a fantasy world. But Owen was real."

The night after Hart died, *Raw* was devoted to the late athlete. His fellow wrestlers spoke about him not as the characters they played but as people who had lost a friend. Many cried without embarrassment as they remembered traveling and joking with the wrestler. Ric Flair was reportedly so touched as he watched the program that he expressed the hope that WCW would give him a similar tribute when he died.

But Bruce Hart believed that the WWF used Owen's friends to make the company look sympathetic: "The wrestlers were being exploited. The comments were from the heart, but they were being exploited because they loved Owen."

Pro Wrestling

Martha Hart, widow of Owen, gives her mother-in-law, Helen, a hug during the family's press conference following Owen's death. Owen's father, Stu, is seated and his brother, Bret, stands behind.

Owen's sister Ellie commented, "Frankly, wrestling was getting so far out and my poor brother, Owen, was a sacrifice for the ratings. That's how I look at it."

Not surprisingly, Bret was also critical of the WWF, wondering why Owen had to be lowered from the ceiling at all. "I feel my heart ache and eyes begin to sting when I think why wasn't I there to protect you . . . to question if this was really necessary," Bret wrote in a newspaper column to his late brother. "Shame on you, Vince McMahon."

Some of Owen's supporters were also offended by the fact that even though the WWF canceled matches in the week following the accident, the pay-per-view match continued after the wrestler's deadly fall. McMahon's response was that Hart was such a dedicated performer that he would not have wanted the event to end. "I'm sure members of the Hart family would concur with me that he would want the show to go on," he said.

People on every side of the conflict poured into Calgary eight days after the accident to say goodbye to the wrestler. The funeral included 13 limousines and 72 cars, along with three buses rented by the WWF bearing the slogans, "We Love You, Owen," and "We Miss You, Owen." Vince McMahon and about 30 WWF wrestlers sat together, not far from Alberta premier Ralph Klein and Calgary mayor Al Duerr. Former WWF stars Hulk Hogan and the Ultimate Warrior also attended, along with the last surviving Von Erich brother, Kevin, and his mother, Doris.

Outside, between 1,500 and 3,000 mourners listened to the service over loudspeakers. "I would like to say that I loved him, I loved him, I loved him, and I miss him," said Owen's widow, Martha, his high school sweetheart and mother of his children, Athena and Oje. "He was my whole world. I don't know how to say goodbye."

For Bret, the occasion was not just an opportunity to remember his brother but also to reflect on the business that had defined his life. "Owen, I loved wrestling with you," he wrote. ". . . Everyone has a song in their heart. Our family's has always been professional wrestling. The hardest aspect of it was always the never-ending loneliness. In reflection of that, both you and I understood from the very start that we were singing a very sad song. But neither of us, even at this dark hour, are ashamed at having sung that song."

Further Reading

Much of the information for this book came from articles published in Dave Meltzer's *Wrestling Observer* newsletter, based in Campbell, California, as well as interviews conducted by the author for various publications, including the *World Wrestling Federation Magazine* and the WWF's *Raw* magazine.

In addition, he recommends the following books:

Albano, Captain Lou, and Bert Randolph Sugar. *The Complete Idiot's Guide to Pro Wrestling.* New York: Macmillan, 1999.

Foley, Mick. *Mankind, Have a Nice Day.* New York: ReganBooks, 1999.

Greenberg, Keith Elliot. *Jesse Ventura.* Minneapolis: Lerner Publications Company, 1999.

Johnson, Dwayne "The Rock." *The Rock Says.* New York: ReganBooks, 2000.

Lewin, Ted. *I Was a Teenage Wrestler.* New York: Orchard, 1993.

Meltzer, Dave. *Tributes.* Carrbora, NC: Powerbomb Publishing, 1999.

Photograph Acknowledgments

The photographs in this book are reproduced by permission of: © Steven E. Sutton/Duomo, p. 2; © John Barrett/Globe Photos, Inc., pp. 6, 104; Corbis, p. 8; © Gregory Pace/Corbis Sygma, p. 9; © Gianni Dagli Orti/Corbis, p. 10; Library of Congress (LC-D416-664), p. 13, (LC-USF 33-021209-M3), p. 14; Courtesy of Norman Kietzer, pp. 15, 16, 17, 18, 19, 21, 23, 24, 26, 30, 31, 32, 33, 34, 35, 36, 38, 39, 40, 41, 42, 43, 48, 49, 50, 51, 52, 54, 55, 58, 61, 62, 63, 64, 66, 67, 68, 70, 72, 73, 76, 78, 80, 83, 85, 86, 92, 93, 94, 99, 108, 114, 118, 119, 120, 121; Corbis/Bettmann, pp. 22, 27, 28; UPI/Corbis-Bettmann, pp. 44, 56; © Mark Solomon/Corbis, p. 47; Duquesnay/Sygma, p. 75; Reuters/Peter Jones/Archive Photos, pp. 88, 90; AP/Wide World Photos, pp. 95, 102, 115, 116, 124; © Ethan Miller/Corbis, p. 96; ©John Barrett/Globe Photos, Inc., p. 104; © Marko Shark/Corbis, p. 107; © Lynn Goldsmith/Corbis, p. 110; © Fitzroy Barrett/Globe Photos, Inc., p. 111.

Front cover photograph, AP/Wide World Photos. Front cover background photograph and back cover photograph, courtesy of Norman Kietzer.

Index

Ali, Muhammad, 55, 74–75, 78

All-Japan Pro Wrestling, 73

American Wrestling Association (AWA), 40, 52, 59, 98, 114

Andre the Giant (real name Andre Rene Rousimoff), 48, 51, 52, 57

Austin, Stone Cold Steve (real name Steve Williams), 7, 8–9, 105, 109–112

Baba, Shohei, 72–73, 75, 78, 84

Bischoff, Eric, 98–99, 105

Brody, Bruiser (real name Frank Goodish) 80–82, 84, 86

Burke, Mildred (real name Mildred Bliss), 31–34

carnivals, 11–14, 31, 32

"Clash of Champions," 67

criticism of professional wrestling, 8, 113

Crockett, Jim, 60, 63, 65, 97

European wrestling, 38

Extreme Championship Wrestling (ECW) 7, 105–106

Fabulous Moolah (real name Lillian Ellison) 30, 35, 54

Flair, Ric (real name Richard Fliehr) 60, 61–62, 63, 65, 78, 94–95, 99

football connections, 18, 23, 62, 82, 102, 109, 114

Gagne, Verne, 23, 24, 40, 52–53, 98

Goldberg, Bill, 102–103

Gorgeous George (real name George Raymond Wagner) 22, 24–29

Gorgeous Ladies of Wrestling (GLOW), 35

Gotch, Frank, 15, 16, 39

Graham, Superstar Billy, 50, 91, 92–93, 114

"Great American Bash," 65

Hackenschmidt, George 15, 16, 39

Hart, Bret "Hit Man," 8, 107–108, 110, 122–123, 124–125

Hart, Owen, 108, 117–119, 122–123, 125

Hogan, Hulk (real name Terry Gene Bollea): 8; 44; 48; vs. Andre the Giant, 52; childhood, 49; debut as Terry "the Hulk" Boulder, 50; as Hollywood Hulk Hogan, 101; as Incredible Hulk Hogan, 50; in Japan, 52, 53; loss to Goldberg, 103; match against Ric Flair, 94–95; match on MTV, 54; move to WCW, 99; movie and television background, 49; New World Order, 96–97, 101; as Sterling Golden, 50; steroid scandal, 93, 95; in "WrestleMania III,"

57; in "WrestleMania VI," 89–90; in "WrestleMania VII," 91; in "WrestleMania," 54–55

Inoki, Antonio, 12, 73–76, 78, 84, 119

Invader No. 1 (real name Jose Gonzales), 84, 85, 86–87

Junkyard Dog, 48, 49

Kowalski, Wladek "Killer," 23, 82

Lauper, Cyndi, 53–54

Lewis, Ed "Strangler" (real name Robert Herman Julius Friedlich), 17, 18

Londos, Jim (real name Chris Theophelos), 19, 20

lucha libre, 76–77, 79

Mankind (real name Mick Foley), 9, 104–105, 106, 113

McMahon, Vince, Jr., 8–9, 45–48, 57, 59, 93, 94–95, 98, 99, 107–108, 113

McMahon, Vince, Sr., 41, 45, 48, 51, 53, 82

Monday Night Raw, 100. *See also Raw is War*

Monday Nitro, 100

Mondt, Toots, 15, 17, 18, 41

Mr. T, 54–55, 56

Muchnick, Sam, 37, 39, 40, 41

Muldoon, William, 14–15

National Wrestling Alliance (NWA), 27, 39, 59, 66–67, 98
New Japan Pro Wrestling, 73
New World Order (N. W. O.), 97, 101, 102, 106

Piper, Rowdy Roddy, 48, 54, 55, 56, 92, 99–100

Raw is War, 100, 112, 123
Rhodes, Dusty, 63
Richter, Wendi, 35, 54
Rikidozan (real name Kim Sin-Nak), 70–72
Rock (real name Dwayne Johnson) 6, 7, 9,
Rodman, Dennis, 101–102
Rogers, Nature Boy Buddy, 40–43, 62–63;
"Royal Rumble," 67

Sammartino, Bruno, 42–43, 57, 73, 92, 93
Savage, Randy "Macho Man," 60–61, 66, 99
Sergeant Slaughter, 58–59, 90–91
Snuka, Jimmy "Superfly," 48, 84
"Starcade," 65–66
steroids, 91–95
"Summer Slam," 115, 122

television: cable, 7, 48, 55, 66–67, 97, 112; closed-circuit, 55; MTV, 54; network, 23, 57; pay-per-view, 7, 55, 57, 65, 67, 91; visual effects, 47
territory system, 37, 39, 48, 53
Thesz, Lou, 20–21, 27, 36–37, 39–40, 71
Tiger Mask (real name Sotoru Sayama), 68–69, 76–77, 78

Ultimate Warrior (real name Jim Hellwig), 89–90

Ventura, Jesse (real name James Janos), 114–115
Von Erich, Fritz (real name Jack Adkisson), 82–83, 120–121

World Championship Wrestling (WCW): acquisition by Ted Turner, 97–98; acquisition of Bret "Hit Man" Hart, 107–108; addition of Hulk Hogan and other WWF stars, 99–100; creation of *Monday Nitro*, 100; creation of New World Order, 101; popularity of, 7; reaction to criticism, 8; reaction to ECW, 106; rise of Goldberg, 102–103; rivalry with WWF, 100–101;
World Wide Wrestling Federation (WWWF), 42–43, 46, 47, 82. *See also* World Wrestling Federation
World Wrestling Council, 81, 87
World Wrestling Federation (WWF): accidental death of Owen Hart, 117–118; beginning as World Wide Wrestling Federation, 42, 45; competition, 59–60, 65, 66–67, 97; creation of "Royal Rumble," 67; creation of "Survivor Series," 65; creation of "WrestleMania," 54–55; creation of *Monday Night Raw*, 100; disagreement

with New Japan Pro Wrestling, 75–76; enforcers, 12; feud with Bret "Hit Man" Hart, 107–109; introduction of Hulk Hogan, 49–50, 52; introduction of Stone Cold Steve Austin, 109, 112; involvement of Jesse Ventura, 114–115; molestation scandal, 93–94; name change, 47; popularity of, 7, 112, 125; raids of other territories' talents, 48; reaction to criticism, 8, 113, 124–125; reaction to ECW, 106; rivalry with WCW, 98–101, 106; rock and roll connections, 52, 53–54; steroids scandal, 91–95; success of *Raw*, 112; use of cable television, 48, 66–67; use of pay-per-view televised events, 55, 57, 66–67; Vince McMahon Jr.'s purchase of, 47
"WrestleMania IV," 67
"WrestleMania VI," 89
"WrestleMania VII," 91
"WrestleMania X," 122
"WrestleMania XIV," 112
"WrestleMania XV," 7–9
"WrestleMania," 54–55, 65
wrestling styles, 11, 12, 13, 77

Zahorian, George, 91, 92–93